WHO OPEN
THE DOOR?

CARI DIEHL

i

Contents

Introduction

Who Opened the Door? Is the sequel to my first book, Shut the Door, which took place during 2015 to 2016. My family had gone through a lot that year. It all began with my father falling so deathly ill that there was no hope of recovery. As a critical care nurse, my skills would have been wasted if I didn't use them for my own father in his time of need. I was granted family medical leave from work to go help him once he had been placed on home hospice, and I traveled to Ohio to take care of him. My heart was even more grieved because I had lost my mom only three years prior. She was my best friend; we were very close, and I could talk to her about anything. Now, my father, who would do anything to protect and provide for his family, was critically ill, and my heart was deeply saddened. He was very family-oriented, and there was never any doubt how much he loved each of his children. Thankfully, we were able to come together and take care of him in his final moments. After three months, he passed away in the comfort of his own home.

During this same time, our dog, Bingo, was very sick. We took him to the vet due to a broken leg, but once he was examined, we found out he had cancer that caused his bones to be weak – which is what most likely is what caused his leg to break in the first place. Bingo was a big part of our family. He gave unconditional love endlessly, and was always so happy to see us. Whenever we came home, he would greet us excitedly by wagging his tail and jumping up and down. I loved coming home from a hard day at work and talking to him; it seemed as if he understood my feelings and what I was saying. After a while, Bingo began having seizures as well. It was hard to watch him deteriorate, but we did everything we could to care for him and keep him comfortable. After a few months, he passed away.

Two or three months after I returned from Ohio to Maryland, my son, Joseph, had a psychotic episode and ended up in the ICU at the hospital where I worked as a nurse. We are still not sure exactly what caused this event, but at one point during Joseph's episode, my husband Bob stated, "If I believed in demonic possession, this is exactly what it would look like." Joseph was seeing and hearing things that were not there. It was the most horrible thing we have ever gone through as a family. Given everything that had led up to this point, my heart could not handle anything more. During this time, we had the support of the Williams, a family who went to the Church of Christ with us. The Williams' names were Dana and Mark, and they were married with three adult sons around Joseph's age. The Williams knew about deliverance ministry, which they taught me about during this tough time. When Joseph was on his way home from the hospital, they prayed with him to receive Jesus Christ as Lord and Savior, and he did.

Even though my son Joseph gave his life to Christ, he still had a long way to grow in Christ. Joseph eventually stopped taking the medication that was prescribed to him during his psychotic episode, and he has not needed any medication since. He went back to his previous job and has not had any psychotic breaks or emotional issues since. Thank God. However, I still wanted more for my family; I wanted my husband and my other son, John, to also know the intimacy of God through Christ Jesus. I wanted us all to walk in the path of righteousness and not destruction. John had issues with marijuana – in fact, he had been in trouble with the law twice before age eighteen. After each run-in with the law, he went to rehab. I actually found out later that while I was in Ohio, John was in rehab for the third time.

The only reason I found out about it is because a couple months after I returned to Maryland, I found a bill from the rehab facility. When I asked Bob about it, he told me that John had been caught with marijuana by the police and had to go to rehab again. He explained that he hadn't told me because he thought I was already emotionally exhausted with everything else that had happened in the last six months, and he didn't want to add to that. By coincidence, it just so happened that I was usually working on the days that John had rehab, so even once I got back home from Ohio, I was unaware of what was going on.

When I found this out, I actually laughed, because there was a day when I could not find John, and I asked Joseph, "Where is your brother," to which he responded, "He's at rehab." I honestly thought Joseph had another mental break, and my heart sank even more. I corrected him and said, "He doesn't go to rehab." Joseph just let the conversation end there, but it turned out he was right – that was John's last day in rehab. Despite all the struggle, I felt like things were coming to a close and I could finally shut the door on that chapter of my life. I was ready to start the next chapter and move forward in my relationship with Christ. As they say – when one door closes, another opens. I could never have imagined what was in store for me behind the next open door.

Chapter 1

A Sense
Of Hope

I desperately wanted my family to be unified in Christ Jesus; I knew that with Christ, they would lead better lives, and I wanted the best for my family. So, I started to seek God more by praying and fasting. I also began to read more books about deliverance. At this time, the only people in my life who knew anything about deliverance were the Williams – friends of mine from the Church of Christ. The Church of Christ neither believed in nor practiced deliverance, but the church leaders were unaware that the Williams were meeting with our peers and spreading the word about deliverance.

As a mother, it hurt me to see the bad choices my sons were making, and to realize they were not where God wanted them to be. Oh, how they had reaped what they had sown! I so deeply wanted to get my family off the path of destruction and onto the path of their destiny with the Lord. Even though Joseph had come a long way, he still had a long way to go. My heart was battling with anxiety over everything in my life, and I knew the only chance for help had to come from God. Yet, when I sought help from the Church of Christ, they didn't even pray with me – instead, they simply told me to seek professional counseling. But God had plans for me and my family: to prosper us and not to harm us (Jeremiah 29:11). I was ready to do everything I could to get my family on the right path of life and bring us into alignment with God's predestined plan for us.

A few years before all this, in one of the hospitals I previously worked at, there were monitor techs. The monitor techs sat in a room of monitors that displayed critically ill patients' heart rhythms and other stats. It was the tech monitor's job to call and alert the floor nurse if a patient had gone into a lethal rhythm or if a patient was off the monitor – then the nurse would go check on that patient. Before work, I would go into the monitor tech room and pray with the monitor techs who were Christians. We would pray for each other and for the patients in the hospital. One of the monitor techs was an Ethiopian man named Bebe. We grew in the word of God together and he told me I should fast, pray, and speak in tongues. He even lent me a book, Fasting: Opening the Door to a Deeper, More Intimate, More Powerful Relationship with God by Jentezen Franklin.

Immediately after receiving the book, I read through it and fasted for three days. On the last night of my fast, I saw in a dream that God wrote three sentences in the sky: 1. Pray for wisdom, 2. Pray for revelation, 3. You reap what you sow. This third sentence upset me; it made me realize that all the hardships my family had been experiencing were the result of me reaping what I had sown. Lately, I had been overwhelmed with frustration and contention, as Bob and I were having intense disagreements and could not seem to connect. Because of this, I threw myself into my work – and while it meant I wasn't dealing with my husband, I wouldn't realize until later that it also meant I wasn't spending much time with my children. In trying to escape my problems at home, I spent far too much time with my friends and coworkers. I would spend long hours at work, and then instead of heading home to be with my family, I would go out for dinner and a drink or two. In my mind, I was not sinning because I was not getting drunk. I would learn later that I was wrong.

After realizing that I was reaping what I had sown, I decided to put my best foot forward in trying to identify the causes of my issues and come up with plans to fix them. I felt disconnected from my family, especially my husband, who did not have an active relationship with God through Jesus. He could not understand my deep intimacies towards Jesus – especially how Jesus died for me on the cross and took all my sins away. All I wanted was for us to see eye to eye, and I hoped deeply that we could share the same passion. Occasionally when we were out together, I felt compelled to minister the gospel to people that we had just met. However, I knew it displeased Bob. It was my desire that we would co-minister the gospel of Jesus Christ to the lost – to share in spiritual experiences about God. Sometimes I would even fantasize about what it would be like to have a husband that loved God and wanted to walk in God's purpose for his life. I needed to figure out how to move us forward to common ground.

My continual prayer was for God to help my family out with this situation. Soon after, some help showed up in the form of a friend. I ended up forming a bond with the secretary where I worked. Her name was Maserya, and she knew everything that was going on in my life, including the psychotic episode my son Joseph experienced. Maserya was actually working in the ICU when Joseph was admitted. We had grown close, and her compassion for me once moved her to say, "I wish you could meet with my pastor." My heart jumped at the opportunity. She knew what I was dealing with and thought meeting her pastor was a good idea. I trusted her judgement. It felt like my prayers might finally be answered. I was desperate for change and eager to move forward in any way I could. I thanked her and told her I would love to meet her pastor. As luck would have it, her pastor was going to have midnight prayer at his house that very Friday.

Maserya's family was from Sierra Leone and so was her pastor. The church was an African church. She seemed surprised when I said I would go, but when it comes to Jesus, I have no prejudices – especially if there is someone who is willing to help when one is in a crisis. Though this was all very new to me and I was unfamiliar with midnight prayer, I was appreciative for the opportunity. When I drove to the pastor's house that Friday night, Maserya called me on the way there to tell me that she was running late and would not be there to greet me. I showed up on time. It was dark outside, and nervousness began to grip me as I walked up to the house by myself. Once I reached the door, I knocked, but there was no answer. I waited a few minutes and I knocked again; this time, the door opened. Behind it stood a middle-aged African man. He was in very colorful tribal attire made of intricate bright orange, maroon, and black print.

Initially, he opened the door wide and welcoming, but once he saw me, a middle-aged white woman, he was puzzled as to why I was there, and closed the door a little.

He asked, "How can I help you?" I explained that I was Maserya's friend and that she invited me to attend midnight prayer. He smiled and politely invited me in. The night prayer session was being held in the basement and he guided me to an empty seat there. After a few moments of waiting for others to arrive, the pastor began to pray. This type of prayer was very different from anything I was used to. First, people prayed in tongues, to which I was not accustomed. Second, when they did pray with words, it flowed freely out of their mouths, as if they did not have to think about what they were praying. It had such depth and meaning. The presence of God was palpable; I felt tingling and warmth throughout my body, and I gained a sense of peace as I felt my depression leave me.

During the prayer session, the pastor was prophesying over people to let them know what God was revealing to him about their lives. When he got to me, he said, "you believe, but you don't put your whole trust in God." I couldn't deny that it was more accurate than I cared to admit. He told me God would perform miracles in my life and he advised me not to go back into "the dark room." I interpreted that as not to allow myself to fall back into a depression. He also told me to believe in the definition of the word FAITH. Accurate again – faith and belief were two concepts I seemed to have forgotten about, yet they are how we reach the Kingdom of God.

Delving into deliverance ministry was refreshing. It gave me a sense of hope I hadn't felt in a long time. I felt like there was a real possibility to turn my situation around – it seemed like there was someone who not only knew how to help, but actually wanted to help me. I felt like I was among people who truly cared. Maserya showed up a little later and caught the rest of the prophecies that the pastor spoke over everybody. I can't remember what time people started to leave, but I know that even though it was the very early hours of the morning, we all felt rejuvenated, revitalized, and connected to the Lord. After receiving our prophecies, everyone had a sense of purpose for themselves in the Kingdom of God.

Chapter 2

The
Dark Room

I had been in a very dark place, and I never recognized it until the pastor said it. But I'm glad he did, because he offered hope in Christ. I started to realize that if I was going to be an agent of change for my family, I had to first change myself. Just as the pastor had said, I was lacking faith and belief. No matter what I did, I couldn't shake how deeply that had resonated with me. The more I reflected on it, the more I understood that the roots of where this came from were deeper than just myself. I sought guidance from my church, but unfortunately, I didn't find the answers I was looking for. When I reached out, the pastor's wife simply told me to seek professional counseling. While it was disheartening, her response made me realize I needed more help than my church could give.

The next time I worked with Maserya, she told me her pastor had suggested that I meet with him and do some counseling. It was perfect timing! Grateful for the help, I eagerly told her that I would love to meet with him. She gave me his phone number right then and there. Soon after, I called to arrange an appointment with him. Interestingly, Maserya stopped working on my unit shortly after I started to meet with her pastor. She was only there for a couple of months. I really believe it was the hand of God that put her there only for that short amount of time so I would connect with her pastor.

My first meeting with the pastor was in his office at church. Confessing all problems, I went into detail about everything that was going on in my life. I told him I truly felt like I was in a hopeless situation, and I brought him up to speed concerning all the recent tragedies my family had experienced. We began with the death of my father and worked our way up through the events of Joseph's psychotic episode. It all had been truly difficult to deal with, but Joseph's turmoil had a visible permanent reminder; the grief Joseph was in had sparked him to get evil tattoos – ones that nearly covered his entire back and both of his arms. They held sinister depictions of graveyards, skeletons, and snakes. He also got tattoos on his wrists that made them look like they had been violently slashed open. The pastor and I went over these details for some time, but I was glad to be able to report that once Joseph had healed, he professed Jesus as Lord, and got a tattoo of Jesus on his back to symbolize his new beginning.

I got a tattoo the day my father passed away: "Jesus is Lord," written in cursive – but I did not divulge this to the pastor. Though I felt deeply about it at the time, I do look back and worry that this may have been an open door for the enemy to come into. According to Leviticus 19:28, KJV "Ye shall not make any cuttings in your flesh for the dead, nor print any marks upon you: I am the Lord." I had read this verse before but believed that it was from the Old Testament, which was before Christ, and as such, did not apply to me. I have since learned that tattoos can cause us to enter into a blood covenant with the person doing the tattoo and open a gateway to demonic activity.

To add to fuel to the fire that seemed to be raging out of control, my younger son was hanging around a bad crowd of people and smoking pot a majority of the time. It was to the point where he had gotten in trouble with the law on more than one occasion. I confided in the pastor that I felt very overwhelmed by everything that was going on, and that I was depressed. I told him that when I went to the midnight prayer, I began to feel more positive about my situation – especially when he had prophesied over me. I felt like God truly was showing him what I was going through, and the prophecy he spoke over me gave me hope that things in my life would turn around for good. The pastor told me that he loves to see God work in people's lives and bring forth testimonies. He shared some great testimonies of similar situations. He prayed with me and set up a time to meet the following week, but not before giving me the following scriptures to memorize:

"Then he answered and spake unto me, saying, This is the word of the LORD unto Zerubbabel, saying, Not by might, nor by power, but by my spirit, saith the LORD of hosts." Zechariah 4:6 KJV

"Before I formed thee in the belly I knew thee; and before thou camest forth out of the womb I sanctified thee, and I ordained thee a prophet unto the nations." Jeremiah 1:5 KJV

"The thief cometh not, but for to steal, and to kill, and to destroy: I am come that they might have life,

and that they might have it more abundantly."
John 10:10 KJV

"But the God of all grace, who hath called us unto
his eternal glory by Christ Jesus, after that ye
have suffered a while, make you perfect,
stablish, strengthen, settle you. 11To Him be
glory and dominion for ever and ever. Amen."
1 Peter 5:10-11 KJV

These were not the typical Scriptures I was used to memorizing, but I was eager to learn and move forward with Pastor Chris. When we met the following week, he prayed scriptures over me and for my household and my family. As he prayed for my children and my husband to follow Christ, he prayed the scripture Zechariah 4:6, "Not by might nor by power but by my Spirit says the Lord." I genuinely started to believe in what he was praying, and I began to delight in the Lord again. It was much different from when I had gone to the Williams' for help; while they knew a little about deliverance, they were still very much involved with the Church of Christ, which did not believe in deliverance or healing ministries. They did their best to help me and my family as much as they could, but I needed somebody that truly understood deliverance and actively worked with it.

Unfortunately, a lot of churches twist scripture when trying to teach it. For instance, the Church of Christ didn't even touch upon the teachings of deliverance and miracles. A lot of people suffer in the Church of Christ due to this lack of knowledge. I silently suffered with anxiety in that church alongside many fellow believers – something that could have been alleviated with the inclusion and proper teaching of deliverance and miracles in the church. There are numerous scriptures about these topics, and I recognized them when I would come across them, I just didn't think they would ever apply to me. There was a time when a pastor from the Church of Christ preached, "miracles are few and far between and that's why they are called miracles." Well, with Jesus, they are not few and far between. We are supposed to be the light of the world. I've often wondered if maybe it's because there are few and far between of God's children who are actually walking in the way of Jesus, that miracles are so "rare."

"Very truly I tell you, whoever believes in me will do the work I have been doing, and they will do even greater things than these, because I am going to the father." John 14:12 NIV

We should be doing greater things than Christ, not less. Let's look at what Christ did.

"And behold, a woman of Canaan came from that region and cried out to Him, saying, 'Have mercy on me, O Lord, Son of David! My daughter is severely demon-possessed.'
23 But He answered her not a word. And His disciples came and urged Him, saying, 'Send her away, for she cries out after us.' 24 But He answered and said, 'I was not sent except to the lost sheep of the house of Israel.' 25 Then she

*came and worshiped Him, saying, 'Lord, help me!'
26 But He answered and said, 'It is not*

*good to take the children's bread and throw it to the
little dogs.' 27 And she said, 'Yes, Lord, yet even
the little dogs eat the crumbs which fall from their
masters' table.' 28 Then Jesus answered and said
to her, 'O woman, great is your faith! Let it be to
you as you desire.' And her daughter was healed
from that very hour." Matthew 15:22-28 NKJV*

Deliverance is the children's bread; it is for us – for the people of God. We can be influenced and demonized by demons. If we are true disciples of Jesus Christ, born again, we cannot be possessed, for the Holy Spirit is in us. When this is so, demons can't affect us and be a part of our bodies. This woman of Canaan went to Christ Jesus for help, it did not state the age of her child. Christ still helped her. She interceded for her daughter, and Jesus answered her request. I knew Christ could help me and my family.

Other scriptures that confirm to do deliverance:

*"And these signs will follow those who believe: In
My name they will cast out demons; they will speak
in new tongues;" Mark 16:17 NKJV*

*"But Jesus rebuking him, saying, 'be silent and
come out of him!'" Mark 1:25 NKJV*

I started meeting with the pastor regularly, and he taught me how to pray deliverance and warfare prayers. Each time we prayed I felt strengthened, encouraged, and hopeful. During this time, most of the focus was on me rather than

those around me, like my family. I felt a little guilty at first, but learned that it was okay. I needed to change myself and look towards God rather than my circumstances. I needed to first be set free from my own bondages of doubt, fear, anxiety, and lack of faith. This was a process. I had to become strong in Christ in order to help the rest of my family to be free.

Pastor Chris held a prayer line at five a.m., Monday through Saturday. This is where everybody participating would get on a group phone call and pray. In this case, we would listen to the pastor pray first, and then we would all pray together after him. Every morning, I joined the prayer line and was very faithful to it. The pastor's focus was about faith. Just like the scripture is written:

"So then faith cometh by hearing, and hearing by the word of God." Romans 10:37 KJV

His emphasis was on hearing the word in order to build our faith. When he prayed, he would use scripture, but he also taught the importance of hearing testimonies from one another – which increased our faith, and helped us to overcome any disbelief.

"Remind Me (of your merits with a thorough report), let us plead and argue our case together; State your position, that you may be proved right." Isaiah 43:26 Amplified Bible (AMP)

When we pray and bring God's word to Him, we bring Him His own word, which He cannot go against, and we plead:

"Therefore I say unto you, What things soever ye desire, when ye pray, believe that ye receive them, and ye shall have them.
He taught us the importance of worshipping, before praying and coming to God. As scripture is written " Mark 11:24 KJV

"But thou art holy, O thou that inhabitest the praises of Israel." Psalm 22:3 KJV

This is letting us know that God is there with us when we praise and worship him; it's like having a direct line to God through Christ Jesus.

One Saturday, the pastor had a get-together to promote his prayer line at another church that wasn't part of where he normally pastored. I invited the Williams, and they agreed. I picked them up and we all went to the church together. The pastor preached and then prayed. The Williams were blown away by the movement of God – the level of prayer was so powerful, and I could tell they were revitalized too. In fact, the Williams made an appointment with Pastor Chris to meet with him that week. Before we knew it, we were all on the prayer line together at five a.m. Monday through Saturday. After that, Pastor Chris started a faith clinic on Saturday mornings from ten a.m. to twelve p.m. as well. We were all there and would spend the first hour worshiping God, and the next hour was in teaching, preaching, and prayer. It was all very powerful.

Every week, people had testimonies – women that were barren became pregnant, and other such miraculous truths. I shared a few of my testimonies as well, including the time when Pastor Chris prayed for my son John to be released from the bad crowd he had been hanging around that caused him to make poor life choices. Pastor Chris prayed for them to leave John alone, and within a couple weeks, one of them had moved to California, another had moved hours away to go to school, and the rest dispersed elsewhere. I believed Pastor Chris was given the gift of faith; whatever he prayed for, the people received.

"To another faith by the same Spirit; to another the gifts of healing by the same Spirit;" 1 Corinthians 12:9 KJV

Around this time, my husband Bob was complaining of loud ringing in his ear. He was frustrated by it and found it very distracting. It became a big source of irritation for him. I told him that he needed to follow up with a neurologist because the symptom could indicate a brain tumor.

He eventually did follow up with the neurologist and had an MRI. He then was diagnosed with a benign brain tumor, schwannoma. It was very small, but if the neurosurgeon operated on it, Bob could potentially lose his hearing. He ultimately chose not to have it operated on, and after a couple months of praying, the loud noise subsided. My husband and I would read the book of Psalms and he said that it helped quiet the noise in his ear. Even though he is Jewish and not a Christian, his faith is familiar with the book of Psalms. I was delighted to share in these moments with him, as he enjoyed reading the book of Psalms and it really seemed to help him.

I remember one dream I had during this time – all of a sudden my hair grew so fast that I felt overwhelmed by it. Pastor Chris said this meant that my glory was increasing; I was growing stronger in my faith and belief by the word of God, worship, and prayer. I truly felt invincible with Jesus Christ, and that all things were possible. I could not wait to see what God had in store for me and my family next. I was ready to leave that dark room, and shut the door behind me.

Chapter 3

A Calling

Around the end of September, nearly a month after meeting Pastor Chris, I went to the grocery store to buy salmon. I was going to host dinner for some friends from the Church of Christ, including the Williams, and another close acquaintance named Grace. I went to a local grocery store and I was so excited about Jesus and all that He was doing in my life that I shared it with the man who was selling me the salmon. He was a tall, middle-aged African man with a stocky build, around age fifty. His name was Peter, and it turned out that he loved the Lord as well. During our conversation it came out that he does street preaching. He shared some scripture with me, and my heart was touched.

My heart jumped within me because I knew that I had been called to evangelize. I recalled a dream I had before I became a Christian where Jesus asked me to evangelize, and I knew now was the time to follow through. "Next time you go street preaching, can I come along with you?" I asked Peter. I wanted to share the goodness of Jesus Christ more than anything. He agreed eagerly and advised me of where he would preach every Thursday and Friday afternoon. It felt like God ordained this meeting, though I did not ask God or seek God for the answer. I just believed that this is what I was supposed to do.

Before long, the day came that I was to meet up with Peter so we could go street preaching together. I met him at a shopping plaza where all the stores were outside. It was invigorating; I found that I loved walking up to strangers and having deep conversations with them about Jesus Christ. It was nice to be out evangelizing with somebody that I felt had the same enthusiasm about Jesus that I did. There was something about Peter that I felt connected to, because of his love for Christ. This man had to have a deep passion for Jesus, the way he evangelized with such boldness. It moved my heart. After we were done evangelizing that day, he invited me to his church.

Accepting his invitation, I went to Peter's church the following Sunday. It was a small church, with a congregation of roughly forty people, nearly all of which were from Africa and spoke French in addition to English. As soon as I walked in, I was heartily greeted by multiple people. One man came up to me and called me by my name when he introduced himself. It puzzled me that he knew who I was. When I asked how he knew, he stated, "Oh, the bishop told me you were coming and to expect you." At that moment, Peter came up to greet me. As I was left wondering who the bishop was, Peter led me to sit down in a chair in the second row of pews. Then he went up to the front of the church and started to worship and sing to God. There was a band on a stage behind him and the music was beautiful. We all sang and praised Jesus. After praise and worship, Peter preached a wonderful message about the heart of Jesus.

After he was done preaching, he introduced me to the church. He said of me, "I think she's going to really help turn this church around." He asked me to come up to the front of the church, and then he had the congregation stretch out their hands toward me and pray over me and my family. They blessed us. Once the service was over, he introduced me to his sons, both of whom played instruments in the band during worship. He also introduced me to his beautiful wife, Lillian. After introductions were over, I asked Peter if he was the bishop and he answered yes. We laughed together. It was really nice to meet everybody and to be around a group of people that loved Jesus as much as I did.

Meanwhile, I continued counseling with Pastor Chris, and we talked about how Peter and I would go street preaching. I told the pastor about some of the encounters I had with various people coming to Christ, and I invited him to come to Bishop Peter's church. I gave him the same invitations that we passed out when we went street preaching, and I asked him if he would call the bishop to make some sort of connection with him. He told me that if God told him to call that he would do so, though he said he did not feel led to call at that time. Even so, Pastor Chris was excited for me. I was excited about my new journey as well, and I was eager to continue learning faith and prayer under Pastor Chris.

"Praying always with all prayer and supplication in the spirit, and watch thereunto with all perseverance and supplication for all Saints;"
Ephesians 6:18 KJV

Thanks to Pastor Chris, I was growing in knowing God more. Through worshipping and praying, I began experiencing manifestation of His presence. My body would tingle all over, and I felt incredibly joyful. I was happiest during this time. It felt like I was really about God's purposes when I was doing street evangelism a couple times a week with Peter. It felt good to be active in the Lord's work, and I wanted to do as much as I could. Eventually, I stopped going to counseling with Pastor Chris, and instead focused more on the prayer line each morning, Monday through Saturday. Then on Saturdays from ten a.m. to twelve p.m., I started to participate in the Faith Clinic more regularly as well. I was beyond happy to be a part of something bigger than myself. I was witnessing so many powerful testimonies: immigrants in need were miraculously receiving their citizenship papers so they could stay in America, and the gravely ill were being healed. I so loved to see God move. It was an exciting time.

One of my favorite scriptures is:
*"And they overcame him by the blood of the
Lamb, and by the word of their testimony; and
they loved not their lives unto the death."*
Revelation 12:11 KJV

Testimonies are extremely important because we overcome Satan by the blood of the lamb and the word of our testimony. When I would do street preaching with Peter, I would see lives changed – I remember one experience in particular where I was getting ready to greet a woman being dropped off at work by her teenage sons, but she looked so angry. I knew this wasn't a good time to talk to her, so I figured I would strike up a conversation with one of her sons instead. The son that was driving the car was smoking and listening to violent music.

As the mother was getting out of the car, I turned toward her son and told him that God had special plans for him and that he needs to turn his life around. He looked at me, dumbfounded. I told him that the enemy was trying to steal, kill, and destroy him – but Jesus wanted to give him life more abundantly. The mother started to cry and she thanked me. The son was very responsive to the message, and I prayed with him and his mother before she went into work. It was very special.

Chapter 4

Increase Knowledge

I was on a mission to understand deliverance at its highest level in order to help set captives free – especially my family. I wanted to increase my knowledge about God and His power of deliverance. I wanted the full gifts of the Spirit. Scripture 2 Corinthians 1:20 NKJV states, "For all the promises of God in him are yes, and in him Amen, to the glory of God through us." This was truly my mission: to inherit all that I could for me and my family because my Father who art in heaven is my Father and I love Him.

While Pastor Chris's ministry was faith centered, Bishop Peter's ministry focused on deliverance and evangelism. I slowly stopped counseling with Pastor Chris in order to give more of my time to learning deliverance. I felt a very deep connection with Peter. In fact, I started to have thoughts enter my mind like, "I wish my husband loved Christ the way Peter loves Christ," and at times I wondered what it would be like to be married to a man who really was on fire for Jesus. Yes, even thoughts about Peter and myself entered my mind. Still, I knew this wasn't right – so I pushed those thoughts aside. Regardless, I looked forward to the days we went out evangelizing. I would confide in him what was stirring in my heart about my family, and he started opening up about his life too.

On different occasions he would share pieces of his life, allowing me to know who he was on a more intimate level. I was so intrigued. One time he explained that hc was in his second marriage and that unfortunately his first wife had died of cancer. His children were from his first wife. I loved getting to know him, but what intrigued me the most was what I found out a few months later. It turns out that he was actually raised in a Satanic cult in Africa, and it was Jesus Christ who got him out. In my mind, I believed if anybody truly knew about deliverance it would be Peter; because he had a background of being in a Satanic cult, he must know everything. He had an incredibly compelling personal testimony. I felt like God was connecting me to him so I could learn more about deliverance to help me and my family.

In mid-October, I got the idea to have a get-together. On Wednesday, I invited a group of people over for a cookout the following Saturday evening. I invited the Williams and Grace, Peter and his family, and a few others from the church. I knew I had to start getting my house in order, and what better way than to have guests over because it forced me to clean up. When Saturday came around, I spent the day cleaning the house and preparing food. My house still had a lot of stuff in it and needed to be decluttered, but on such short notice I had no time for that. I didn't mind though, because I was so excited that my husband and sons were getting to meet some of these people from my new church.

I prepared a simple cookout meal of grilled chicken and some side dishes. The Williams were the first to arrive. Then Peter and his family came along with their friend George. They knew George from their time back in Africa. He was about twenty-six years old and played guitar for the worship team at church. George lived with Peter and his wife Lillian, and they referred to George as their son. Peter's daughter-in-law also came with her six-month-old baby. I introduced everybody to one another as they came into my house.

After entering the living room, Lilian glanced over her surroundings. As she looked at the area of clutter in the corner, another guest from church, Dana, noticed her facial expression and immediately defended me by saying, "Cari has been going through a lot lately, and she's been working on getting her house in order. It's actually come a long way since my husband and I anointed the house only a few months ago." Almost everyone I knew was aware of what my family had been through. Even at this point, we were all still in a low-grade depression and trying to find our way back to normalcy. It was very hard at this time in our lives – even maintaining the upkeep of the house was difficult. Lilian nodded her head in acknowledgment, and I went outside to get the chicken off the grill while my husband welcomed the rest of the guests.

Everyone was talking when I brought the food into the house. I announced that the food was ready, and I asked my husband, Bob, to get Joseph. Our youngest son John was not home that night. Joseph came out from his bedroom to the dining room, and I introduced him to George and Lilian. What they noticed first were his tattoos – the ones that made it seem like his wrists had been slit. You could tell they were afraid, but compassionate. They engaged in some polite conversation with Joseph until I announced food was ready, and we all went to fill up our plates. Once everyone got what they wanted, we returned to the living room to sit down and eat.

George and Joseph sat in chairs next to each other. Lillian and her daughter-in-law sat on the couch, taking turns holding the baby throughout dinner time. The rest of us sat in chairs around the room. I was delighted to see that a conversation had sparked between George and Joseph since they were close to the same age. As we ate, we all continued to talk. Mark had some business in Africa, so he talked to Lillian about that.

Toward the end of the evening, Lilian began talking about the church and how she and her husband worked in deliverance ministry. We were all excited because this is what we had been waiting for; we needed someone who knew about the subject more than we did. Mark talked heavily to Lilian about the ministry, and she gave him Peter's phone number so he could set up a time for them to help with their situation and receive deliverance. Overall, it was a successful evening. I was meeting more people that knew about true deliverance ministries, and it made my heart swell to see my family engaged at the cookout as well. At the end, we all stood up, held hands, and prayed.

Not long after the cookout, I dreamt that I walked into a room and I saw a man who was very frail and sick. He was sitting in a chair and was too weak to stand up. Then a woman entered. She wore a red, silk corset trimmed with black lace. Her attire resembled that of a Burlesque theater girl outfit. She also had a fancy hat with feathers in it. She started to sing and move towards this man. He used all his energy to stand up to greet her. She stood next to him and then they kissed each other. As they were kissing, he was sucking the life-force out of her. She became weaker and weaker, until the next thing I knew, she began to morph into a fish. She allowed him to suck her energy out of her so he could live. They asked if I could help them, to which I said I would. Then I woke up and spent the next while trying to figure out what this extremely bizarre dream meant.

When I went to Wednesday counseling session with Peter, I told him all about the dream. I was expecting him to say, "It's only a dream, just forget about it." But I was shocked by his reaction. He said, "Do you know who this is?" When I did not answer right away, he excitedly raised his voice and asked again, "Do you know who it is!?" I insisted I did not know who it was. I thought this was very strange because when I went to the Church of Christ, they basically told us not to pay attention to our dreams. I figured he would say the same, but his reaction was intense and strange. I tried to reflect more deeply on my dream.

There seemed to be more to my dream than I could understand. Deep down, I felt like it had something to do with Peter. I tried to focus and remember what the man in my dream looked like, but I couldn't remember the exact details. I dug deeper, trying to recall defining features for comparison. I couldn't remember if the man in my dream was black or white, though I was certain he was a middle-aged man. Peter was also a middle-aged man. I couldn't really remember too much of the singing woman either, except that she looked like a show-girl from the 1920s. These details were so far-fetched, I was almost inclined to blow them off and let the dream fade away, but the way Peter reacted, I knew this had more meaning.

This got me to thinking about all the dreams I'd had throughout my life. So many dreams I'd had that could have truly meant something, but I brushed them aside because the Church of Christ told its followers not to pay any attention to their dreams. The church would quote the bible verse Jeremiah 23:31-32 NKJV "31Behold, I am against the prophets," says the Lord, "who use their tongues and say, 'He says.' 32Behold, I am against those who prophesy false dreams," says the Lord, "and tell them, and cause My people to err by their lies and by their recklessness." They would also quote Ecclesiastes 5:7 KJV "For in the multitude of dreams and many words there are also divers vanities: but fear thou God."

However, there so many other scriptures in the Bible that talk about the importance of dreams and how God would talk to people in their dreams: 1Samuel 28:15, Acts 2:17, Daniel 1:17, Genesis 20:3, Genesis 40:8, Genesis 42:9, Numbers 12:6, Joel 2:28, Matthew 2:13, and more. Looking back, it bothered me to realize that when I started going to the Church of Christ, I pretty much stopped paying attention to my dreams – even those that really stuck with me. It made me especially frustrated because my dreams are what led me to Jesus Christ in the first place.

Shortly after that realization, I stopped going to the Church of Christ all together, and instead I continued to participate even more diligently on the prayer line with Pastor Chris. Around this same time, the Williams wrote a letter to the Church of Christ explaining the importance of deliverance and the gift of tongues. The Church of Christ asked them to leave the church and explained that deliverance was not the doctrine of the church. The Williams then began attending Pastor Chris's Church with me.

The next time Peter and I went out evangelizing, I started preaching loudly in the shopping plaza about how people need Jesus and how Satan is coming into families and destroying them. I would preach, "The thief comes to steal, kill, and destroy. Did the enemy come and wreak havoc in your household? If he did, Jesus came to set you and your household free so that you may live life abundantly!" People stopped to listen. The more I yelled about Jesus and how the Kingdom of God was near, the more I felt God's presence, which encouraged me to peach more. Each time I went out evangelizing, my message became clearer. It evolved and I added to it with each visit to the plaza.

After that, I preached, "Repent, for the Kingdom of God is near you!" The following day, I preached, "How is your household? How is your family? Is Satan in the household? For the thief comes to steal, kill and destroy. Is Satan destroying your household, your children, and your family?" Walking up and down the plaza, as if I had bullhorn, I'd shout, "Come to Jesus and he can help make every crooked way straight. Jesus is the only way, and he truly loves you. He died on the cross for you. He paid for all your sins when he died on the cross and rose to life on the third day."

Before long, a friend from the Church of Christ saw me while I was out evangelizing. She came up to me and incredulously asked, "What are you doing?" I explained to her why I was out preaching, and then I introduced her to Peter. It turned out that she and Peter were from the same African country. She started to cry tears of sadness because I told her I'd left the church of Christ. I explained to her all the reasons why I had left, including that they did not really adhere to the gospels when it came to deliverance. She continued to cry, and I started to cry too. I knew what she was thinking – that I was wrong, and I had lost my salvation. The Church of Christ believes that they are the only church living out the gospels, and that all the other churches are not truly about God's business. However, I was growing in deliverance, and I was happy to share that experience.

At this time, I started doing more counseling with Peter on Wednesdays, before mid-week meeting. When we would meet for counseling, it would be the two of us alone in the church. Before we got started in the counseling sessions, he would ask me to go up to the altar at the front of the church and pray to God. I did feel somewhat uncomfortable with the situation, but not enough to stop meeting with him. During one of my first counseling sessions, I confided in Peter that I believed I still needed some deliverance. We did a soul analysis for me – this is an analysis of all the things my ancestors and I had done wrong against God: the sins, transgressions, and iniquities.

We started to work on the list of all my sins and all the sins of my forefathers that I was aware of. It is very important to repent of your ancestors' sins, transgressions, and iniquities, and also to pray for the blood of Jesus Christ of Nazareth to cleanse those sins, transgressions, and iniquities. Some examples of sins to repent are: stealing, lying, witchcraft, unforgiveness, hatred, sexual perversion, adultery, and the like. You need to command the spirits that have legal rights to you – due to the sins of your ancestors – to leave.

Quotes out of the book, Urban Disciple, by Tialie Simpson. Pages 8, 19, and 29:

"Sin is the willful or ignorant breaking of God's statutes, precepts, rules, and or laws. It is being contrary to His nature of love, compassion, care, concern for all living things according to His standard and not our own. He is our Creator and Father. As our Creator, He knows how He designed our bodies therefore He knows what will be a harm to our bodies and what will fuel it or heal it. Furthermore, He designed the universe with laws and principles. In order to function or operate grow and live within it and prosper we have to follow His rules concerning it. As our Father and marshal, He sets the boundaries for us stay and abide within. Once we crossthe

boundaries, we do what is called transgress(ion)."

Transgression: the act or process of breaking a law or moral rule, or an example of this:
pesha

Phonetic Spelling: (peh'-shah) breach of trust, rebellion, rebellious, rebellious act, rebellious acts, transgression, transgressions.

Iniquity: gross injustice: WICKEDNESS
Greek: anomia., "lawlessness" (a, negative, nomos, "law"), is used in a way which indicates the meaning as being lawlessness or wickedness. Its usual rendering in the NT is "iniquity," which lit. means unrighteousness."

When there is a sin, transgression, or iniquity that someone commits, it allows demons to have legal rights to that person if they do not repent and allow the blood of Jesus to cleanse them. There is a spirit behind the sin that influences the transgressor; then it starts to influence the next generation as well, and it becomes a generational curse. This is why you can see family blood lines continually having the same sins such as alcoholism, gluttony, sexual perversion, witchcraft, and so on.

If no one in the family has gone through deliverance, these entities hang around you and your bloodline, trying to get you and your family members to engage in similar sins and iniquities. In the church of Christ, I repented of my sins and was baptized. Yet, I still had demons affecting me; this is why I had struggled so much in being a born again believer – I was plagued with anxiety and depression as a generational curse. I learned that it wasn't just my own transgressions I needed to repent. This is why you can see cases where people become born again Christians but don't deal with the bloodline and end up finding out that their own children didn't follow Christ, but took up the sins of their forefathers and ancestors instead.

This is what Peter and I kept working on during our Wednesday counseling sessions. One Wednesday, he was praying over me with deliverance prayers – he was speaking in tongues and commanding different spirits to leave me – and I actually started to vomit. Peter's son had been working in the area to set up chairs for the Church service later that evening. When I got sick, he stopped setting up and quickly grabbed a bucket and paper towels for me. They both looked surprised, but we continued the session. It was very powerful. I could tell it was a turning point in healing from my generational curses.

Almost every Wednesday from that point forward, Peter and I had a standing appointment for counseling. Sometimes he would ask if he could be my pastor. I would respond, "If you're really following Jesus Christ, then yes." I found this to be such an odd question. I was counseling with him and evangelizing with him – why did I have to verbally agree to this too? Later, Grace also started doing counseling with Peter. Grace and I would even occasionally do counseling with Peter together on

Wednesday evenings. She and I both wanted to learn to speak in tongues, so we would all go over scriptures about it, such as: Mark 16:17, Acts 2:4, Acts 19:6, 1 Corinthians 1:5, 1 Corinthians 12:8 –11, 1 Corinthians 14:2, 1 Corinthians 14:23, and 1 Corinthians 14: 27–28.

Peter would lay his hands on us and pray over us, so that the Holy Spirit would come upon us and we could speak in tongues. He would also walk around us and speak in tongues himself. Grace and I both would feel the manifestation of the Holy Spirit. We would feel a tingling sensation throughout our bodies, but we still did not start speaking in tongues. After a while of trying like this, we stopped doing sessions together. To be honest, I preferred it when Grace did not share the counseling session with me. Even though Grace was a close friend of mine, I wanted more time to talk about my own personal issues and my family.

I felt very connected to Peter when I was confiding in him all the things that were going on in my life. It felt good that he not only seemed to understand, but that he also seemed genuinely interested. I believed that he truly wanted to help me and my family to follow Christ Jesus. We continued to evangelize together every Thursday. I really enjoyed being out on the street in the shopping center, preaching Jesus. When we were doing this, I felt the Holy Spirit stronger and more intensely than ever before – my whole body would have this tingling sensation and words would be pouring out of my mouth with power. Usually, I would stand in the middle of the shopping center and start yelling, "The kingdom of God is at hand; repent and be baptized!"

I would share to the world Galatians 5:19-22, and any other scriptures that came to me. I would say, "God loves you so much that he gave his only begotten son for you, to die on the cross so that you may have eternal life," and I would also preach how Jesus set the captives free. Calling out, I would ask, "Is there anybody here captive by sin that needs to be free? Let me preach to you the good news of Jesus Christ!" Peter was amazed at the way I preached with such boldness. He told me, "Once you start speaking in tongues, you are going to be so powerful." I couldn't wait.

During one of our evangelizing outings, a woman came before us. She was white with blond hair and a thin frame. She looked to be in her mid-thirties, and was disheveled in appearance. She was hanging around the shopping center, and there was something odd about her behavior. My guess is she was schizophrenic. She did not like being touched and she did not want anybody to know who she was. Peter would always give her a little food to eat from various restaurants around the area. He was trying to reach out to her, but she never even allowed him to know her name. Peter introduced me to her and asked if I could try to talk to her and make a deeper connection than he had been able to. He asked me to pray and preach to her the way I had so passionately done for others in the shopping center. He told me he saw how I could speak to people's hearts, and wished the same connection for this woman.

Peter had been reaching out to this woman for a long time and was hoping to finally bridge that gap. As we discussed her, he advised me that in all this time, he had only been able to get a few small details from her and knew that she did not work. I engaged with her, and since she didn't want to tell me her name, I asked her if it was okay if I gave her a name. She said that was fine, so I gave her the name Sarah, which she accepted. I asked her if it was okay to pray with her, which she also accepted. I prayed with her and asked God for his presence. I continued to pray for God to touch her heart and to take away all the pain and hurt in her heart. I asked for her heart to be filled with the Holy Spirit. In between praying, I tried to ask questions and connect with her, but if I tried to talk to her directly, she still would just shut down. She would allow me to say just a simple prayer, but if I did much more than that she would walk away.

Still, I never lost hope. I kept trying with her, as I did with others. I really enjoyed some of these intimate encounters with the people that I met on the street. I could tell right away if people were open and receptive to me approaching them. If they averted their gaze or walked away from me, I would not pursue them; I would just let them walk on by. But if I would walk up to somebody and they made eye contact with me, then I knew that they were open to talking to me. I would usually start asking them basic questions, like "who are you," and "what do you do for a living," trying to figure out their need for Jesus.

Most people have a need for Jesus – whether it's for themselves personally or for a loved one. There were so many people I met during this time, I can't remember each and every one of them, but I especially loved to encounter the youth. I would fearlessly approach groups of teenagers. Some of them were very open and receptive to hearing about Jesus. I'd usually talk about how God has a great destiny for them and how Satan wants to steal it away. Then I would go into my mind and ask the Holy Spirit, "What is their destiny?" Sometimes I would get an idea and I would ask them if that was something they ever thought about. There were times I was right, and they would always be impressed. If it wasn't something they had thought about, now perhaps they had something to consider. I let them know that the Holy Spirit was showing me, and I would hand out invitations to church and little booklets about the Word of God.

I remained steadfast in my routine: Wednesday night counseling with Peter before mid-week church service, then evangelizing Thursday and occasionally some Fridays with Peter. In our counseling sessions, we continued going over scriptures about the Holy Spirit. We would pray on these scriptures:

"and I will pray the Father, and He will give you another Helper, that He may abide with you forever— 17The Spirit of truth, whom the world cannot receive, because it neither sees Him nor knows Him; but you know Him, for He dwells with you and will be in you. 18I will not leave you orphans; I will come to you." John 14:16-18 NKJV

"However, when He the Spirit of truth, has come, He will guide you into all truth; for he will not speak on his own authority, but whatever He hears he will speak; and He will tell you things to come. 14He will glorify me, for He will take of what is mine and declare it to you. 15All things that the Father has are mine. Therefore, I said that He will take of mine and declare it to you." John 16:13-15 NKJV

"So Jesus said to them again, 'Peace to you! As the Father has sent Me, I also send you.' 22And when he had said this, he breathed on them, and said to them, 'Receive the Holy Spirit.'" John 20:21-22 NKJV

After we would discuss some of these scriptures, Peter would start to pray over me; he would begin speaking in tongues and ask the Holy Spirit to come into me. He would blow on me and repeat, "Receive ye Holy Spirit, receive ye Holy Spirit." We continued this until later in the evening when mid-week service would start. Despite all this, I did not speak in tongues. I was getting frustrated. The Church of Christ believed that the gifts of the Holy Spirit had passed away – they would advise that people who spoke in tongues were making it up or that it was demonic. I had years of these teachings in my mind and I knew I had to overcome it. Peter would give me assignments to work on after counseling, and I would study more scripture on the Holy Spirit:

"But you shall receive power when the Holy Spirit has come upon you; and you shall be witnesses to Me in Jerusalem, and Judea and Samaria, and to the end of the earth." Acts 1:8 NKJV

"When the Day of Pentecost had fully come, they were all with one accord in one place. 2And suddenly there came a sound from heaven, as of a rushing mighty wind, and it filled the whole house where they were sitting. 3Then there appeared to them divided tongues, as of fire, and one sat upon each of them. 4And they were all filled with the Holy Spirit and began to speak with other tongues, as the Spirit gave them utterance." Acts 2:1-4 NKJV

Again, we would pray for me to speak in tongues and he would speak in tongues and recite scriptures. He would ask the Holy Spirit to come upon me. After a while of trying, I felt my right arm levitating and a tingling sensation spread throughout my whole body. Peter encouraged me to speak in tongues and mimic his words, which I did – but still I did not feel the power of the Holy Spirit speaking through me. However, when he was praying over me, I sensed the Holy Spirit surrounding me and him. When he instructed me to receive the Holy Spirit, I could feel that I truly was in a state of receiving this time. I hoped great things were in store.

The next time we went to evangelize, I saw Sarah and I spoke with her. I prayed over her for the Holy Spirit to touch her heart and help her through her pain. While we had been at this for a little while now, she still didn't want anyone getting very close to her. It seemed like she could only handle a little bit of prayer and a little bit of talking each time; anything more and she would walk away. But I kept on evangelizing in the shopping plaza. I would preach loudly to anyone who would listen – "How is your household? How is your family? The devil comes to steal, kill, and destroy. Has the devil been affecting you and your family? Is the devil stealing from you? Is the devil killing and destroying your life? Jesus Christ has come to give your life back – and to give it more abundantly!" I would continue quoting scripture and preaching the good news of Jesus Christ.

On special occasions after service, the church would have celebrations where the ministers and their spouses would sit in front of the church at a table designated for them. This was a place of importance, and those sat at the table were served by wait-staff. The table was dressed up with a white tablecloth and had plenty of food and drinks on it. It was West African potluck style; everyone brought their own special dishes, all made with love. It was impressive. Aside from the food and placing set for the ministers and their spouses, the rest of the congregation had to wait in line to get their food, which was set up like a buffet. While the food and display was lovely, somewhere in my conscience, this whole situation didn't sit quite right with me. Would Jesus set himself apart to be waited on, I wondered.

One Sunday, they asked me to join them at the table to eat. This was because I would go out and Street preach with Peter, although I was not ordained in that position. When they included me, I almost started to cry – I was literally holding back tears as I joined them, I felt so honored to sit with them. That particular Sunday, the Williams were attending church along with Grace. I was excited for them to share in this experience, and for them to get to eat the amazing food. I still didn't know what to make of it all, though. It almost seemed like too much, and to add to that, Peter's wife gave me a beautiful African dress. It was royal blue with gold trim, and it was akin to those that the other women in the congregation would wear on special occasions like this. I was happy to feel so included, but the grandeur of it still felt strange.

I couldn't accept the dress without giving something in return, so I insisted on paying Peter's wife for the dress. We made small talk, and I learned that she would sell jewelry and perfume on the side to make a little extra money. She asked me if I might like to purchase anything from her, and I told her that would be fine. We decided to have a get-together on Thursday evening so I could look over what she had. She agreed, and that Thursday she brought her wares to my house. The products she had were nice, but I don't really wear perfume so we focused more on the jewelry. It was mostly costume jewelry but very classy. I bought a couple necklaces with matching earrings. We had a pleasant evening, and I walked her to her car as she left.

The next day as I was going out to my car, I noticed a CD on the ground. It was a CD of worship songs that Peter had made. I contacted his wife, Lilian, to let her know I had it, and she told me that I could keep it. It was a lovely CD full of wonderful worship music. I grew to play it quite frequently and would often play it as I cleaned the house. Around this same time, I started to notice I was having strange dreams again. This time, I dreamt that I had three horns on my head, and I plucked them out one by one. I took this dream to Peter and asked him what it meant. He only shook his head and told me he did not know. After the last set of strange dreams, I didn't want to let this one go. I thought about it deeply and asked him, "Maybe I have sinned and not repented of something?" He nodded and replied, "That could be." Still, I didn't feel satisfied. I was left wondering why I had dreamt I had three horns, and what the significance of plucking them out meant.

Later, I looked it up in the book, *The Divinity Code to Understanding Your Dreams and Visions,* by Adam Thompson and Adrian Beale. On page 381 it shows horns with two representations: 1.) strength, and 2.) power. I found this very interesting, and recalled upon a few bible verses that mention horns:

"For you are the glory of their strength, and by your favor our horn is exalted." Psalm 89:17 (KJV)

"But my horn shall exalt the horn of an unicorn: I shall be anointed with fresh oil." Psalm 92:10 (KJV)

"All the horns of the wicked also will I cut off; but the horns of the righteous shall be exalted. Psalm 75:10 (KJV)

For some reason I was starting to feel spiritually weak. I was noticing the culmination of all the things that had seemed off, or that I had questioned. Looking back, I began to notice that spiritually I lost my strength. I found myself tired and not praying as fervently as I previously was.

Chapter 5

Nothing Like Friends

In early December of 2015, it was starting to get cold outside, so we slowly stopped evangelizing. I would always take the same way to work, and every day I would see homeless people on the way. They were always at the bus stop, and it was a little group of three middle aged African-Americans – two women and one man, all in their fifties to sixties. The man had a wheelchair and appeared to be a little older than either of the women. They spent every night at that bus stop and I would take note of them each morning as I drove to work.

One night I dreamt that there was a snowstorm and God told me that I needed to help them. If I helped them, He would bless me. He also would teach me to grow more in Christ and to help my family. It was a joyous dream, and I was eager to help. By January 2016, the holidays came and went, and the temperature continued dropping as the dead of winter set in. Many times it dropped below freezing. On my way to work one of these bitter mornings, I knew it was time to reach out. I stopped and gave them twenty dollars so they could go into the McDonald's next to the bus stop to warm up and get some food and hot coffee.

When I approached the bus stop, only one of the three were there at the time. It was one of the ladies. I gave her the money and said, "You need to get out of this cold weather and get some coffee." She smiled. I explained that a blizzard was coming, and she took warning. She happened to be reading the Bible when I had approached her, and she kept praising Jesus for the money I had given. She thanked me profusely and explained that the other two were in McDonald's using the restroom. She introduced herself as Esther, and I introduced myself to her as well. We spoke another moment, and then I got back in my car and headed to work.

I was glad to have carried out God's word to me, but then I started to have more bizarre dreams. Sometimes in my dreams, I would have sex with people other than my husband. These dreams made me feel so uncomfortable and guilty. In another of these bizarre dreams, I dreamt that I was swimming in a beautiful river. It was trying to carry me home, but there were rocks in the way. I would try to go around them, but no matter what I did, I couldn't get past them. My heart was breaking because I was trying so desperately to get home, but could not make it past that point.

After a while, I sought out answers on these dreams, and I was able to find helpful interpretations in a book; I found out in a book called Disgracing Water Spirits, By Dr. D.K. Olukoya. On page 53, he says about water spirits:

"Sex in the dream: Another root cause is sex in the dream. The spirit of whoredom pollutes the lives through sex in the dreams. Sexual soul ties are their handiwork. You need to strive and deal with them. Fornication, adultery, lesbianism, masturbtion, oral sex, body exhibition, incest, abortion, uncontrollable sexual desires, etc. are the activities of the spirit of whoredom. Anyone who goes into any of these things may not come out alive. Powers of the water have spread their dragnet

to catch many, using all their sexual hooks."

One example of a water spirit in the Bible is about Dagon who was half man and half fish: a merman, (Judges 16:23, 1 Samuel 5:2-5, 1 Samuel 5:7, 2 Chronicles 10:10)

In the book The Spiritual Warrior's Guide to Defeating Water Spirits by Jennifer LeClaire, on page 153 it states:

"In summary, Dagon wants to capture your heart so it can capture your anointing. Dagon wants your worship so it can displace the presence of God, the source of your anointing in your life. Dagon wants to blind you from the source of who you are and the source of your life. Dagon wants to cut off your authority to pray – he is after your head."

In another strange dream, I dreamt that I was in California on a bus on top of a mountain. I was the only person on the bus. There was a big earthquake and the bus started to fall into a pit that had opened on the mountaintop. I woke up and I asked God what this meant. I prayed about it, and I also told Peter about the dream during our counseling session. Still, all I could think of was that perhaps I was in sin and just did not realize it. As usual, Peter nodded and said, "That could be the cause." I then proceeded to confess any sins to him that I could think of, and repented of them. However, this did not stop these bizarre dreams. In fact, the dreams continued getting worse.

I pressed on. During my days at work, I would have my phone on me, and keep the sound on low, playing worship music. As a nurse in the ICU, a lot of my patients were intubated and sedated; when I would clean them up, I would sing and pray over them. There was one day when a coworker asked me to help clean up her patient who was a homeless guy around age thirty. He was very sickly, had lice, and was HIV positive with AIDS as well. At the time, he was receiving a lot of blood transfusions and was in a coma. She probably knew that nobody else would help her and that as a Christian I am here to serve. She was also a Christian. I agreed to help her clean him up, but only if I could pray over him.

She and I started to clean him up and we both came in agreement that he shall be healed and restored in the mighty name of Jesus Christ. I would plead the blood of Jesus over him and kept praying for complete healing and restoration in the mighty name of Jesus, amen. After we were done, she thanked me and said, "You really know how to pray! I want to learn how to pray like that." All the doctors and nurses expected this patient to die, but he did get better, and he was downgraded to another unit in the hospital to continue to heal.

A month or so later, one of the doctors made a comment as we were eating lunch in the break room. She said, "I can't believe this patient that was previously in ICU is now walking down the hall. Everyone expected him not to make it." She was talking about the patient the other nurse and I had prayed over. I let the doctor know that we had prayed over him. Even though I knew that this doctor was not a Christian, she stated she believed in prayer and faith. She was a little amazed, but I was content in hearing that the patient was making such a good recovery. There have been a handful of other times where I prayed over patients and they received healing. I really enjoyed doing that. If the patient was awake, I would ask them if they wanted prayer. In general, most people would say yes. And so, I would pray.

There was another incident around this time where I had a patient who was from India, and she had two daughters by her bedside. She was intubated and unable to breathe on her own, as she has some chronic issue with her lungs. The respiratory therapist was in her room while I was there, and I asked if they wanted prayer. Her daughters said yes. As I started to pray, the respiratory therapist also started praying and speaking in tongues. We could sense God's presence all around; the daughters sensed it too and were amazed. Their mother ended up getting better and leaving the hospital.

Meanwhile, a couple weeks passed, and the homeless people were still at their bus stop. There had a big blizzard headed our way, and I stopped again to check on them and warn them. I told them a huge snowstorm was about to hit and they needed to seek shelter. Esther advised me that they could not go to shelters, and that shelters were very dangerous. However, she assured me that she had put in a call to somebody they knew to see if they could get any help.

By this time, light snowfall started coming down and Esther asked if she could give me some stuff to hold onto, like their sleeping bags. How could I refuse? I did not want their stuff to get wet or ruined by the weather, especially if it was all they had to keep warm. I agreed and told them I was headed to the hospital – so if they wanted to come along to get out of the cold, they could. The other lady, Debra, ended up coming along with me. When we arrived at the hospital, we went to the cafeteria and I gave her some money to get something to eat. She was content and she sat in the cafeteria a while.

She had her phone and I gave her my number. I had also given Esther my number before we left for the hospital, so we were all able to communicate. I left Debra in the cafeteria and continued about my day at work. Meanwhile, the snow kept coming down. After work, I called Esther to find out what plans had been put in place. She informed me that Debra took the bus and went back to the bus stop. I was concerned because now the snow was coming down fast and starting to get heavy. I asked her if any other progress had been made for them to stay somewhere out of the snowstorm. She advised me that the woman they were trying to get in touch with earlier said they could not stay with her.

I pleaded with her to go to the shelter, but she once again insisted that the shelters were very dangerous and they would not go. My heart sank. What could I do? I felt compelled to help. I told her that I would pick them up and take them to my house. At the same time, my husband called me to make sure I was okay. I told him I believed I would be okay to get home in the snow. He wanted to come and get me since his vehicle did better in this weather, but I insisted that I would be fine.

As I left work, the snow was coming down like an actual blizzard, and it beat down upon me as I scraped the snow off my car. Driving home, there were hardly any cars on the road, and the thick snow made it hard to see. It was a very eerie feeling. I called when I got close to the bus stop, and Esther told me they would be at the McDonald's next door. When I arrived, they said McDonald's had closed, so they were just sitting outside of it. I got the three of them loaded in my car and started heading home. As we drove, we saw police and military vehicles rounding up homeless people to take them to the shelters. One last time, I asked, "Do you want to go with them?"

Esther spoke up as the leader of the group, and she said "No, it's very dangerous in the shelters." I knew she would not go with them. For some reason, they truly feared the shelter. While I was driving home, my husband called a couple times, but I did not pick up because I knew he would be angry that I was bringing homeless strangers into our house. I didn't know how I was going to handle this once I got home, but I would deal with it once I got there.

When I arrived home, my husband came outside to greet me, and I knew he wasn't happy that I hadn't answered his calls. Frustrated, he asked me, "I've been calling you, why didn't you pick up?" I replied, "Because I was bringing home these homeless people that have nowhere to go, and I knew you'd be upset." My husband did not say anything because the group was there with me. I quickly introduced them to Bob. As Debra, Esther and Moses were getting out of the car and toting their stuff into the house, Bob was kind to help carry some of their belongings into the house too. While we guided them into the living room, my husband told me, "It's okay – they can stay for the night, but tomorrow they have to leave."

I took them down into the family room and showed them around. In the family room, we have two couches – one shaped like an L, where the main section pulls out into a bed, and then another sturdy wooden couch that sits on the other side, making the whole thing U-shaped. I told them to make themselves comfortable, and as an act of hospitality, I offered blankets and towels to help them settle in for the night. I also offered to pull out the couch into a bed, but Esther explained they didn't want to do that since they were used to sleeping sitting up on the bus bench.

Debra took the sturdy wooden couch while Esther took the longer part of the sectional and Moses took the shorter part. To make them more comfortable, I turned on the television and I began to press the different menu buttons to demonstrate how it works – explaining how they can access YouTube too. They were really impressed, and they listened to gospel music on YouTube for the entire evening. Later, I invited everybody to come upstairs to the dining room for dinner. We had leftover chicken and I made rice and a salad to go with it. Moses sat at one end of the table and Bob sat at the other end. I introduced my son, Joseph, as he joined us. I asked if Moses could pray over the meal, and he said such a beautiful prayer. Then he thanked Bob and me, and blessed us and our household. He prayed for Joseph, and prophesied into his life. He also prophesied into my life and Bob's life. I enjoyed it, but Bob confided in me later that he found it very strange.

The prayer Moses said over dinner made me cry, it was so beautiful. During the meal, I asked each of them how they came to Christ. Moses started off, and he shared how he didn't have an easy life growing up in Washington D.C.; he was made fun of and bullied. He said he had a lot of anger, but he had an encounter with Jesus Christ, and knew that if he did not follow Jesus, he was going straight to Hell. Esther told her story and then Debra. Each of them had such interesting coming to Christ testimonies.

After dinner, Bob informed them that they would have to leave by tomorrow. They were in agreement and thanked him for allowing them to stay the night. We finished our dinner as we watched the snow come down through the bay window in the dining room. After everyone finished eating, we said goodnight. I headed up to bed thankful that I didn't have to work the next day. As

I got ready for bed, my husband confronted me. He was still unhappy and said, "What were you thinking bringing homeless people into our house? You don't even know who these people are – you don't know if they're dangerous or not!"

I explained to him that I see them at the bus stop on my way to work every day, and I'd observed them for some time now. I let him know I had stopped on occasions to chat with them and give them money. I advised him that they wouldn't go to a shelter and had nowhere to stay. After all this, he simply reiterated, "They have to leave tomorrow." Even though I had a dream to help these people, I wasn't sure if I was handling it the right way. My husband's reaction had me second-guessing the situation. I began to doubt what I had seen in my dream, but I followed through with it anyway. I felt it was better to do it and be wrong, than not to do it at all, only to find out it truly was God's intent.

Because of this internal struggle, it was very hard to sleep at night knowing that they were in close proximity to Joseph's room downstairs. Even though Joseph was an adult, I was still concerned. At one point, in the middle of the night I heard somebody in the kitchen. So, I went down and I saw Esther cleaning. She said that she wanted it to be a surprise and she was trying to be quiet. Relieved and grateful, I returned to bed. That night, I dreamt again that I was having sex with a lot of people. I woke up and asked God to help me.

Morning came and there was so much snow that we couldn't even get out the front door. All the roads were completely covered with snow, and there wasn't a plow in sight. We knew there was no way anybody was leaving today. When Bob and I looked out and saw all the snow piled up, I asked him if they could stay since there was no way they could leave. Bob agreed to let them stay one more night. We were all stuck together in the house, but I was determined to make the best of it, so I went about cooking breakfast for everybody.

I told Esther that they could stay one more night, and she was happy to hear that. She came to help me in the kitchen. We talked a little and she started to pray over me. She began prophesying good things about me; she told me I would be like Kathryn Kuhlman and be an Apostle. It was such a good experience because I never really had anybody prophesy into my life with such power like that before. I admitted that I didn't know who Kathryn Kuhlman was, but the thought of being like an Apostle was intriguing. Esther talked about all the work that Kathryn Kuhlman did for God, and how she was part of different ministries through which she gave glory to God.

I asked Esther about her family, and she told me she had some children and an ex-husband. She explained that her children were all grown up and on their own, and that she later married Moses. She said that she used to be a cop and she talked a little bit about what that experience was like, as well as some other adventures God had led her on. For example, she had traveled all over the place and once ended up moving to Alaska and became a housekeeper for a very influential, wealthy woman. I was fascinated with hearing her life story.

We finished cooking breakfast, and I was a little amazed that we were prepared and had enough food for everybody throughout the time they stayed with us. I was glad. When it was time to eat, Esther called Moses and Debra to come upstairs from the family room and eat. I called Bob and Joseph to come downstairs from the bedrooms to eat as well. We all sat around the table and ate together in the kitchen – except for my son John; he refused to come down for dinner. He was upset that I had taken in this group of homeless people, so he stayed in his room.

After we finished breakfast, everybody left the table, and Esther and I did the dishes. Esther remarked at what a great husband I had. I confided in her that I didn't think I was supposed to have married Bob because right before our wedding, I dreamt that angels came to me and told me not to marry him. In the dream, I asked if I could just be married until I turned thirty, and then I would get a divorce. The angels said they would go ask God. When they returned, they advised me that God said that would be okay. So, I married Bob with the intent that once I turned thirty, we would get divorced. I told Esther that I never did divorce him – and because of that, I felt like I had failed God. I believed God had greater plans for me. She reminded me of God's grace, but in my heart I felt that was not enough.

Esther spent her day cleaning the house, for which I was extremely appreciative. Most people would not allow some stranger coming in as a guest and cleaning their house. My husband was wary, but I didn't have much apprehension. There was really nothing in the house of great value, and anything of concern was either in our bedroom or the office – both of which were off-limits. More than anything, I was happy to be helping these people, and grateful to be getting help around the house in exchange.

While Esther cleaned, Debra and Moses stayed downstairs in the living room watching TV throughout the day. Most of the day went on like this. Esther explained that she didn't want the others to help with anything, because this was basically like a mini-vacation for the three of them, and she wanted to bless the other two. She said she also wanted to bless me by helping out. To me, this was the greatest gift anyone could give; I never seemed to have enough time to get my house in order, let alone keep it that way. I would take any help I could get.

She was very thorough as she cleaned throughout the day, even going so far as to wash the walls. I told her she didn't have to work so hard, but she said she was content to help this way. I felt bad because the bathroom they used while staying in the family room was Joseph's and he never took care of it. Nevertheless, Esther cleaned it all, and even scrubbed the tiles spotless. Once she was done, it was mid-afternoon and we started to hear the plow trucks driving by and clearing the roads. We all looked out the window at the plows, and you could almost sense a collective sigh of relief.

Thank God we would be able to get out soon. Being cooped up in the house together due to the snow had caused a little tension, though never anything enough to be an issue. While we let the plows do their jobs, Esther helped me cook dinner. We got to talking and she told me that while she was cleaning she could feel that there were demons in my house, and that they were accusing me of some dark actions. She also explained that she saw a demon around Joseph's neck. It was truly frightening to hear – and coming from someone I didn't know well, I thought she might be crazy, but I was willing to listen.

I responded by thanking her for letting me know. I thought to myself, the Bible says not to have anything to do with familiar spirits. Nonetheless, I allowed her to continue. We held conversation, and I would try to veer her away from talk of spirits when I could. I told her about evangelizing with Peter, and about the morning prayer line with Pastor Chris. I let her know how extremely helpful these things had been in teaching me how to have faith.

She said that she used to attend Peter's church, and that she believed it was not a good church – that there was something strange about it. I was very offended when she said that, but I tried to remain polite. She could sense my discontent though, yet only offered a bit of advice; she told me, "Before you go to bed at night, ask God about each and every person – he will reveal their truth to you." Our conversation tapered off there, as dinner was ready. We set the table and called everyone to come eat. Again, everyone joined us but John.

While we are eating dinner, Esther told Bob that he was under God's protection because God was going to use him to do something very special. I knew Bob thought right away she was crazy, and I could tell that this interaction solidified that the time our guests were allowed to stay was limited. Moses broke the tension by once again saying a wonderful prayer over the household and for each member of the family. After dinner, my husband announced that he was still concerned about the road conditions, and to my amazement, said that our guests could stay one more night. I learned later that Esther, Moses, and Debra had been praying to be able to stay longer, and God answered their prayer.

That night when I went to bed, I had a dream with Pastor Chris and Peter in it, but it was all jumbled up -- I could not remember much of it. The small details that I could remember were strange; there were two girls and a boy who came out of a toilet and I was cleaning them. I remember specifically cleaning the legs of the boy. This was interesting to me, because I knew Moses had wounds on his leg that Esther would clean and bandage up in the bathroom. Through this dream, I knew God was telling me that I was cleaning these people up.

In the morning, Bob took me to work. Once I was done, he also picked me up in the evening, and from there, he told me we were meeting Debra at the store where she worked, because she ended up going into work that day too. On the way to pick her up, Bob told me he bought some steaks that were on sale and that we were all going to celebrate my birthday together. Bob had really had a change of heart, and it made me so happy. When we got home, Bob cooked dinner, Esther set the table and served the food, and John even ate dinner with us. Once more, Moses prayed over the family, and Esther joined him this time too. It was truly an enjoyable birthday dinner, and it warmed my heart.

The next day, the roads were mostly clear. We assessed the weather conditions while we ate breakfast together, and Bob and I decided it was finally okay for me to drive myself to work. That also meant it was time for our guests to leave. They packed up their belongings, and we all loaded up into my car and headed out. I played the prayer line on the radio with Bluetooth connection from my phone so everyone could hear.

We talked a little as I dropped them off at the bus stop and they unloaded their belongings. The snow was melting and there was slush in the road, but the temperature was in the fifties, and you could tell it was going to be a sunny day. I told Esther that I wanted to pay her to keep helping clean my house. She was happy to hear that and she agreed. We had each other's phone numbers and made a plan to keep in touch. We said our goodbyes and I headed to work.

Chapter 6

Connections

The following Sunday came and it was time for church. My husband needed my car, so he dropped me off. It was someone's birthday at church, so there was a celebration and people brought food. There was a table of food lined up at the back of the church – lots of chicken, fish, side dishes, and beautiful desserts. We had church service in the front, and Peter preached a great message. Afterwards, I was asked again to sit up front at the table with all preachers and evangelists again. I felt so honored. They had servers bring food to the table, so I didn't even have to get up and wait in line. The food was exquisite. Still, I wondered why I was brought up to the front. Though I went out regularly to evangelize with Peter, I didn't quite feel like I belonged up there.

Regardless, I was thankful for the company and the meal. Everyone was sharing about how they got through the blizzard. When it came to be my turn, I recounted how I took in the group of homeless people from the bus stop. Nobody said anything. In fact, almost everybody started to leave the table, and only Peter and I remained. He explained that I should not have taken in homeless people because they are dirty and spiritually unclean. I was confused. I told him that the Bible says we should take in the homeless. At this time, my husband came in to pick me up and someone led him to me and Peter. I introduced them, then Peter invited Bob to sit down and have some food. Bob joined in the conversation and shared his side of how we took in the homeless during the storm. Still, there were no positive reactions. After Bob was done eating, we left.

I felt saddened at how negatively the church had looked down on the homeless, but I knew what was right in my heart. I pressed forward, and focused on what was ahead of me. For my fiftieth birthday, my present was for us to go to Jamaica as a family. There was one week to go before the vacation, and I started to have nightmares. One of those dreams was with my youngest son John. It was related to our upcoming vacation. We were going to Montego Bay, but I dreamed that John went on his own to Negril, Jamaica to buy marijuana.

He was in some sort of building that looked like a bunch of storage units, and he was arguing with a group of people. I followed him and watched from outside the rundown building. Then I heard a gun go off and I knew that John was dead. There was a lady next to me saying, "Aren't you going to cry? They just killed your son, and you're not even crying." I told her that I don't really cry, but I was feeling very numb about it. I was in shock. I thought to myself, I won't believe it until I see a dead body. It was so overwhelming, but it came to me that this nightmare was demonic. I truly believed that the spirits wanted me to agree with them, and if I cried, that would bring the dream to pass – crying would tell the demons it's okay to kill my son. I refused to cry; I wouldn't let them see me or my family suffer.

The next morning, when I woke up, I got dressed and went on the prayer line with Pastor Chris. I told the people on the prayer line what I dreamt. I was advised that I need to cancel the dream so it does not manifest into the physical. So, we did. That same evening, Bishop Peter's church was having an evening prayer line, which I attended and I told them about the dream as well. Right away, Peter started to pray and cancel the dream. After he did that, he suggested coming over to my house and meeting with Bob and me. We agreed to do so that Thursday evening.

Thursday evening rolled around and Peter came to the house to meet with us. We all went into the living room and I offered him something to eat and drink. He only asked for a glass of water; he said he didn't want to eat anything, as he wouldn't be staying long since his wife was at home cooking dinner. Before he sat down, he said he was going to bless the house, and he started to move his hands around like he was tossing a ball. Once he was finished, he took his glass of water and we all sat down.

We had a short conversation and Peter prayed over us. As he stood up and got ready to leave, he happened to look through the dining room window into our backyard. He commented on what a gorgeous yard we had. Our backyard is about a quarter of an acre, surrounded by beautiful mature trees. We asked if he wanted to go out and take a look. He agreed and we all stepped outside. He started praying over the land and doing that hand motion again, and this time he also started speaking in tongues. It was a curious event, but you could truly feel the power of Christ. Once Peter was done, he left. I was hoping he would have some revelation as to what was going on in my home, but he did not share any insight.

There was a respiratory therapist in the hospital that I would work with occasionally, and we would pray together. She showed me the Periscope app and how her church used it. I became so intrigued by it, I was immediately hooked. Any time I had a spare moment, I would watch people on Periscope. I found people preaching, teaching the Word, and praying for others. I would go and watch people prophesy on a level I had never before seen.

Some of my favorite personalities on the app were Kimberly Jones and Bishopnanjo. When they were on Periscope live, I could write comments and they would answer; I would ask for prayer and they would pray for me. Through Kimberly Jones's Periscope page, I met Tialie Simpson, and I started to follow her on Periscope as well. One night I started to watch Tialie's Periscope and I asked her for prayer. She started prophesying into my life. Among other things, she said that I would write books and that I was going to get a new car. This all was so fascinating. I was inspired to get my own Periscope page, and eventually I started a show called "Pray 5 Minutes Before Work."

I kept in contact with Esther, and at the end of February after my vacation there was another snow storm brewing. I asked Bob if we could have them over again because it was going to be bad. Bob had compassion and agreed. Thankfully, I also had a few days off from work, so we could all spend time together. I invited them over, and it was just like before – maybe even better. We picked them up on Thursday evening, ate dinner together and then went to bed. On Friday, Esther started cleaning my house and I told her

I would pay her. As she was cleaning, I asked if she wanted to listen to music. She agreed.

I gathered a bunch of CDs and happened to find Peter's CD of worship. I put that on and started to sing along with it. She emphatically stated that she did not like the music I had chosen. I asked Moses and he said he did not like it either. They said it did not set right in their spirit. Esther suggested playing the Bible on CD instead. So, I did. When evening came, we all ate dinner together except for John. I explained to the group that since the next day was a Saturday, Pastor Chris had the Faith Clinic in the morning, and if they wanted to go with me, they were welcome. They said they would pray about it. The plan was for them to leave our house on Saturday evening when the weather would be better. Once dinner was over, we all went to bed.

In the morning, I began getting ready for the day. I went down to the kitchen to make breakfast for everyone. While I was cooking, Esther approached me and said that they would all go to the Faith Clinic with me. I was so happy. After breakfast, we all left to go to Pastor Chris's house. When we arrived, I introduced them to everyone there. At Faith Clinic, there is a big screen TV and we play Christian music through it while we worship. The majority of our time is spent in worship, and then afterwards we pray.

Pastor Chris usually does not ask for offerings, but this time when we were done praying, he asked everyone for an offering. People all gave what they could. Then he asked if the new guests could come up and introduce them selves. They went up to the front of the room and did so. When they were done, he said, "God wants you to have this money." They started to cry and so did I. When we left Faith Clinic, the sun was shining bright and reflecting off the snow, making it look like the whole yard was glittering. It was a beautiful day.

Once we let, I took the group back to the bus stop. We said our goodbyes, and then I returned home to settle in for the evening. I still struggled with sleeping because the nightmares were getting worse and more perverted. There were dreams where I was having sex with a bunch of people and was tossed around like a rag doll. I would wake up and start praying against it with all my might, but the nightmares were so unnerving, it was as if I was so exhausted that I couldn't even pray. I would also have dreams of constantly eating food. I couldn't understand what it all meant, but it got so bad I was reluctant to even try to sleep anymore. I didn't know what to do, I felt lost. I still struggled with how much stock to put in my dreams, since for all those years my previous church had taught me not to pay any attention to them. But these crazy dreams were increasing, and I knew there had to be more to what was going on.

What was also strange was that I hadn't previously noticed I used to have a sense of Jesus being next to me, as if he was constantly to my right. I always had a sense that he was there, and I took that for granted. After having these nightmares for a while, I finally realized that the sensation of him being close to me was gone. I felt disconnected from

God – I could tell that something was truly missing in my life. Once I realized it was Jesus that was missing, things started to click a little more. The following Sunday at the end of church service, a parishioner came to see Peter but he kept walking away. The parishioner pursued him and kept saying "I'm really having crazy dreams and I need to talk with you," over and over. I thought to myself, wow I'm not the only one who's having crazy dreams. It turned out that this parishioner's name was Tony and he knew Esther, Moses, and Debora.

When I next talked with Esther, I told her everything that was going on and how I was suffering from absolutely bizarre dreams – that they were plaguing me. She told me I needed to get out of Bishop Peter's church. She then explained that she knew somebody in that church named Tony who confided in Esther that he truly believed Peter's wife to be a witch. She explained that Tony would stop by the bus station and they would talk for hours, but they had known each other for years, so she trusted him. I asked Esther if she saw anything in the Spirit about Peter in this church. She paused and she said, "I see a bunch of people arguing with him about scriptures." I wasn't sure what to make of it all; I still felt like the whole thing was a little too out there for me.

The weather started to warm up as spring arrived, and at the beginning of April, Peter said we needed to go out and evangelize again. I was really excited about this. We went back to our usual place. I hesitated to tell Peter about my dreams because they were of a sexual nature, but they were really bothering me at this time, and I could not sense Jesus with me anymore. I eased into conversation with Peter and began to mention I was having dreams in which I was having sex with people who were not my husband. He listened, so I continued. I even told him that I had a dream where a woman showed me her naked body, and her vagina was where her belly button was supposed to be. In the dream, I was stunned; I simply told her, "I don't know what to do with that." It was very strange, especially because I have never been interested in women.

After a moment, Peter looked at me and told me these types of dreams aren't good to have at all. Then he chuckled and told me he didn't know what to do with the information he'd been given. I waited for him to say more, but that seemed to be it. I was surprised he didn't explain to me what any of it might mean, and I was a little frustrated that he didn't elaborate on why these types of dreams were so bad to have. At this time, I didn't yet know about Water Spirits, or as they're also known, Succubus Spirits. You may have heard of an incubus or succubus before. An incubus is a male demon who tries to seduce sleeping women by laying on them. The succubus is the female counterpart, a water spirit.

I also want to mention here that in the book, *Cracking the Dream Code* by Elisha Goodman, on page 62 it states:
    "Dreams of having sex mean you have a spirit
    spouse who will do everything in its power to
    destroy your earthly marriage, just to keep you for
    themselves. They sometimes cause business failure,

get anyone who comes close fired from work, and
even arrange fatal accidents to eliminate all
competition. People who have sex in the dream
are "loaded" with all kinds of spiritual materials
like serpents circulating in their body without
their knowledge, unexplainable health problems,
and routine failure and frustration. They find it
really difficult to have conception and give birth.
Many of them end up being barren ... and running
from place to place for solutions. If they manage to
get married, they find that the finances of the
family disappears suddenly and mysteriously."

Again, at this time I didn't understand all this. However, I was happy to at least get it off my chest and tell Peter what was happening. I had hoped that sharing would be enough to at least make the dreams less – less bizarre, less frequent, just less.

Peter and I went on our way evangelizing at our usual place. I started preaching, "The kingdom of God is near, and you need to repent and be baptized!" I would then start to yell, "How is your household? How is your family? How are your children? Is the enemy destroying them? Jesus is the answer of restoration; he will restore your children and your household!" I talked to a few people about Jesus, and then we were done for the day. As we were leaving, I asked Peter if we could meet for counseling that Wednesday. He agreed.

On Wednesday, I showed up for counseling and I re-iterated that I was still having bizarre dreams. Even the night prior, I had a really strange dream with

Donald Trump in it. I explained that in the dream, Donald Trump approached me and asked, "Would you pray for me?" I told him "I do not do witchcraft prayers." He turned his back and started to walk away from me, but then he turned back and said, "The Bushes are against me." I told Peter how I thought this was all strange, as I knew absolutely nothing about politics. I had so many questions rushing through my mind: *Why am I having dreams with Donald Trump in them? What does all this mean? It's April 2016, Trump has no way of winning the election – is God trying to tell me he wants Trump to be president? I didn't understand. Peter only responded, "Stop thinking about this."*

But I couldn't stop thinking about my dreams. They were plaguing me. I desperately wanted answers. It was becoming increasingly difficult to just shrug off my dreams. Then everything Esther had said popped into my mind. So, I thought I would test the spirits. Referring to 1 John 4:1-3 NKJV "Beloved, do not believe every spirit, but test the Spirits, whether they are of God; because many false prophets have gone out into the world. 2By this you know the Spirit of God: every spirit that confesses that Jesus Christ has come in the flesh is of God, 3and every spirit that does not confess that Jesus Christ has come in the flesh is not of God."

So, then I asked Peter, "Who is Jesus Christ?" He replied, "He is the Son of God." Well that was almost good enough, I thought to myself. I had strength in my spirit and asked again, "What does 1 John 4 say about who Jesus is?" He started to say, "Jesus Christ," but he

was going very slowly, so I interrupted and completed the verse for him. He stared at me with a look of deep questioning. I sensed he could tell I was beginning to not trust him anymore, though his semi-hurt look made me second-guess why I was questioning him so hard.

I could not believe in my heart that he could be a false prophet. I knew he knew the verse, why was I making him recite it? Why did I doubt him? After all, he was raised in a Satanic cult and came to Christ; he probably had one of the best testimonies out there. My head was spinning. In this counseling session, he said, "Your husband is not a Christian and he should not be praying for you." He had said this to me before, but it never made sense. This time I asked, "Where does it say in the Bible that an unbelieving person should not pray for their spouse?" He did not answer.

Also, around this time in April, I asked Esther if I could pay her to come over and clean the house. She agreed but she asked if it could be a day that it rained so they could be out of the rain. I said that was fine. The next day that it rained, I went and got Esther. Moses was with her, but Debra went to work. Later in the day, it stopped raining and Esther and I took a break outside in the backyard. The sun was shining bright. We sat at the picnic table and spent some time on Periscope together.

I introduced her to my show and to the people that I met on the app. She was so intrigued and excited about Periscope, it reminded me of when I was first introduced. She asked if I was still going to Peter's church and re-iterated that she felt there was something strange going on there. I did not respond, but I did think about it for a moment this time. When the day had ended, I took her and Moses back to the bus stop.

I had started to make friends with a woman from my church named Isutu. She was raised Muslim but ended up giving her life to Christ. She started to come over and help me pray. Peter was unaware of this. She prayed for many hours a day, and I asked her to come over and pray over my house. She did. She came over when nobody else was home, and she commanded fire to come down and destroy the enemy in this territory, in Jesus's name amen. She was speaking with such authority – it was very powerful to witness. We went into everybody's bedroom and she kept praying. She would even speak in tongues. I kept praying too. That night, I dreamt a shrouded figure came to me and said "Joseph has evil handwriting on the wall." I didn't really understand what that meant, but I told Isutu.

She came over a week later and we prayed again. We washed Joseph's wall and pleaded the blood of Jesus over it. We prayed to wash off every evil handwriting on his wall, in the name of Jesus. When we had finally exhausted ourselves in prayer, she left and went home. I asked her to keep visiting. I felt like we were doing really good work. Every time she came over, I would give her a financial blessing. In some quiet moments after praying, we would talk about church. She talked about various members in our church, but what struck me was when she said she trusted Peter but did not trust his wife.

When I asked her about her feelings of distrust toward Lillian, she explained that another member of our church believed the pastor's wife was a witch. This was too much for my mind to handle. I couldn't believe I was hearing it for a second time from another source. Were people putting stock in this notion? I didn't know what to believe, but it did make me think of the dream I had earlier when I first started going to Peter's church. I felt compelled to explain the dream to Isutu. I told her, "I dreamt I walked into a room and saw a man who was very weak and sick. He was sitting in a chair and too weak to stand up."

She was intrigued. I continued to explain how in the dream there was a woman who was dressed in a red Burlesque-style dress. She wore a red silk corset with black lace around it and a hat with feathers in it. She started to sing and move towards this man. He used all his energy to stand up to greet her. She stood next to him and then they kissed each other. As they were kissing, he was sucking the energy out of her, and she became weaker and weaker until she turned into a fish. She allowed him to suck her energy so he could live. They asked if I could help them, and I said I would. When I finished telling Isutu all the details, she responded, "That is witchcraft." I couldn't believe it, but before I could ask any questions, we were interrupted by Joseph coming into the house and greeting us.

A few days later, Peter's son, George asked if he could come over to my house because he went to talk to me about something. I agreed. When he came over, we sat down on the couch in the living room, and I asked him what was up. He told me he needed a thousand dollars to

fix his car, and asked me if he could borrow the money. I actually had some money set aside, so I said yes. I went up to my bedroom to get it for him. He was thankful as he accepted it, and told me he would pay it back when he could.

The next few weeks were uneventful, but I continued on the prayer line with Pastor Chris. He talked about how we need to really sacrifice for our miracles to happen. He preached about how Abraham sacrificed Isaac. With everything that had been going on in my life, I felt like I sure could use a miracle. At this time, my husband and I were not getting along at all, and he and I were both easily agitated. I had it in my mind that I needed to leave Bob, and that this would be the best sacrifice. I thought, *maybe God thinks I put my husband ahead of my relationship with Christ.* I wanted to let God know that he was my first love.

I was reminded of my promise to God that I would divorce my husband by the time I was thirty. I felt like this was an opportunity to make up for lost time. Maybe this would get my destiny back on track, whatever my destiny in Christ was. Also in my sacrifice, maybe God would bless me, and everybody in my house would come to Jesus. After having these thoughts, I ended up having a dream that I did leave Bob. With all the dreams I was having, there was some uncertainty, but I believed this one might be a confirmation of what I needed to do next. I talked to Esther on the phone and explained that I felt like I needed to leave my husband. She agreed that it was the right thing to do.

Chapter 7

Completion

By this time, it was early summer of 2016, and I had it in my mind to leave by July seventh. My plan was to leave my husband, quit my job, and move back home to Ohio to be closer to my family. As it neared closer to July, I grew more anxious. I kept having bizarre dreams, but they started to revolve around me leaving. At one point I had a dream that my car got stolen. When I went to the impound lot to get my car back, the lady working there said she couldn't find it and that she would have to go upstairs to use the other computer. I went up with her, and when she looked on that computer, she said, "Oh no. Satan took your car because you're supposed to have a miracle ministry with Pastor Chris." I started to pray, and once I finished, she said "The car is back – it's in front of the building." Then I woke up.

Despite my apprehension and these vivid dreams, I knew I had to follow through with my plan. When I told my brothers and sisters I wanted to leave my husband and come back home, they all agreed that I could stay at our dad's house for as long as I wanted. Preparing for my move back to Ohio, I started to pack my car with clothes and other things that were important to me. I gave three weeks' notice at work that I was leaving, and I began registering to become a nurse in the state of Ohio. I didn't think too much farther ahead about what I would do next, because I was afraid if I thought too much about it, I wouldn't go through with it.

One morning I woke up early and came down to the living room and sat on the couch. I pulled out my phone and got on the prayer line with Pastor Chris. Then I got a text from Peter asking, "Can I come over?" I responded, "Sure," assuming he would then provide the details about when he would be stopping by, but he never responded after that. As the prayer line continued, I fell into a deep sleep. I dreamt the front door opened slightly, and I answered it. There was a man in a white gown with a head covering on the other side of the door. He laid his hands on me and said, "I need to take the copper out of your brain," and then he started speaking in tongues. I woke up after that and was in a haze. I wondered if it was Peter in the white gown since he never got back to me about coming over. I also surmised that the man telling me he had to get the copper out of my brain was due to the fact that we had recently redone our pipes and we used copper piping for the water supply. Regardless, it was bizarre.

Later that week when I went to church, I did not ask Peter why he never responded or came over. I just went about my business. On Wednesday night church service, we were worshipping and praying. We were singing beautiful Christian songs, one of which touched my heart so deeply that I cried out to God. I cried out because Bob and I were going through such a difficult time, and I felt like I was not loved by my husband. I cried and I asked God for help.

That night when I went home, I fell into a deep sleep and had another strange dream. I dreamt there was a large blob-like substance the color of my skin. It stood before me, and in a man's voice it said "I love you." I thought, maybe this is the Holy Spirit telling me He loves me. It felt good to hear somebody say they loved me, and I thought that maybe this came from God because I'd been praying and worshiping. Still though, I could not sense God's presence like I used to. I realized later this was not the Holy Spirit, but I couldn't figure out what it was. Was it perhaps Peter or a demon visiting me under the guise of the spirit?

Getting closer to my time of departure for Ohio, my husband informed me that we needed to go to Costco to get his mom a new TV set. My husband did not have a Costco membership; the membership was in my name, and with it you can add one guest to your account. As a goodwill gesture, I added his mother to my account. I had one card to our account and his mother had the other card. So, either I had to go or she had to go, and since this was a gift for her, I would have to be the one to go. He talked about going on Saturday which was July seventh, and that was the day that I was going to leave. I prayed about it and asked God what to do, and I just trusted in Him that somehow things were going to work out.

I knew I couldn't stay because I already quit my job, and my car was packed. I worked on July sixth – it was my last day at work. Once I finished my shift, I was very tired and went straight to bed after getting home. Then I woke up at four that morning. Needing a pep talk, I said to myself, "All I need to do is get in my car and leave.

My car is already packed. I have clothes set aside. Everything is set. It's now or never." So, I got out of bed, picked up the clothes and shoes I planned on wearing for the day, and quietly went to the downstairs bathroom to change. Then I got in my car and left. I played worship songs in the car and was singing along – I kept going and didn't allow myself to second-guess what I had just done. I kept my mind focused on what I felt like I needed to do.

As I was leaving Maryland, I was singing and praising God when suddenly I started to throw up. I rolled down my window, spitting up as I drove along the highway. I felt like deliverance was occurring. As I came into Pennsylvania, I was still anxious, but feeling a little better. I stopped to fill up on gas, grab coffee, and get a bite to eat. I reached Ohio around nine that morning, and I called my siblings to let them know I was there. I started to think about what I should do now that I had actually followed through with my plan. I decided that above all else I needed to fast, pray, and seek God. Prior to leaving, I applied for a nursing license in Ohio so I could find a job there; I did receive my nursing license for Ohio, but I was not ready to look for a job right off the bat. I wanted to focus on seeking God and sensing His presence again.

Once I started to settle in, I called my husband and let him know that I would not be going to Costco to get his mother's TV set. He asked me if I got called into work. I said no – I decided to go to Ohio, and I told him I had quit my job. He said, "Cari what are you doing?" I explained to him that I always felt like our marriage was not supposed to happen. I told him about the dream where the angels said I should not marry him, and we agreed that I would divorce him by the time I turned thirty. I also reminded him that this was not the first time I had told him this.

Bob said that he wanted me back. At that time, I declined and I decided not to pick up any of my phone calls until I got more clarity from God. I didn't use my phone except to participate in the morning prayer line and to talk to my friend Shannon. We prayed together every day. She was the first person I called when I arrived at my father's house. I told her I had made it there safely, and that I was going to fast for three days while I sought God and figured out what to do next. She was a big support to me, and I confided in her about all my crazy dreams. She told me, "If you're eating in your dreams that's a very bad sign." I knew fasting was the right choice.

Shannon told me to watch Prophet Ugo Ezeji on Periscope. He was a deliverance minister. I had a lot of dreams where people were force-feeding me to eat. At this time, I didn't realize that it was bad. But later I read in the book, Cracking the Dream Code by Elisha Goodman on page 58-59:

"Dreams of eating means that your spirit man is very dull and weak and is not strong enough to withstand Satanic activities against you. In fact, they could even feed you with human flesh and blood in the dream this way, and by the time you wake up, you find yourself physically ill. This is a

popular method of planting sickness and incurable dieases in the lives of people. Jesus said: "While men slept, the enemy came and sowed tares." The tares include spiritual poison in the dream through food. You will need to vomit the evil consumption ... and then lash out with holy anger against evil night caterers like this: "You evil caterers feeding me in the name, I command you to eat your own flesh and drink your own blood in the name of Jesus." This is an advanced warfare prayer that has its basis in the scripture, in case you are wondering. In the book of Isaiah chapter 49 verses 25-26. You now see how certain scriptures that are not taught a lot in most places could hold the key to your victory and deliverance from bad dreams, among other things."

Over the next three days, I fasted, prayed, worshipped God, and steadfastly read my Bible. This may seem boring, but I understood that it was not about obligation, but about my relationship with God. I needed answers and I needed direction – I questioned whether I was even truly saved at this point. I was still having crazy dreams and was lacking the presence of Jesus next to me – I knew I needed to seek God whole-heartedly.

and you will seek me and find me, when you search for   me with all your heart." Jeremiah 29:13 NKJV

And those who know your name will put their trust in you; for you, Lord, have not forsaken those who seek you." Psalm 9:10 NKJV

While I was in Ohio, Peter tried to call me, but I blocked his phone calls. His wife also called me, and I blocked her calls too. I didn't pick up the phone for nearly anyone, including my husband. The only people I talked to were Shannon, Pastor Chris and the Williams. During my first call with Pastor Chris after I arrived in Ohio, I told him that when he preached about making a sacrifice, I thought the best thing to do for my situation was to show God that I put Him first by putting an end to my marriage. I also explained to him that I felt like Bob and I should have never been married in the first place.

Pastor Chris actually laughed a little bit and said another woman on the prayer line did the same thing. After we talked about my situation, he said what I was doing was wrong and then gave me some scriptures to read. However, in my heart of hearts I felt like this was what I needed to do, for many reasons. I also spoke to the Williams and they told me the same thing – that what I was doing was wrong and I needed to go back home. But I wasn't ready to go back home.

After three days of fasting, I dreamt vividly of the number ten. I believed God was telling me that I needed to fast for ten days, so I continued praying, fasting, worshipping, and reading the Bible. After a week I finally spoke to my husband; he was still upset and asked me to come back. He let me know that he missed me and that my children had missed me too. We would even pray over the phone together.

While I was in Ohio, I had my iPad and my phone with me. I spent every morning from five to six on the prayer line with Pastor Chris. I spent a lot of time using Periscope and watching YouTube videos. I was studying Kathryn Kuhlman and other famous evangelists with healing ministries. I would also watch YouTube videos about satanic cults and symbols they use, trying to educate myself on what to look out for, or what I may have encountered already. I began to create a structure for myself between the prayer line, praying on the phone with Shannon every day, and studying.

Per Shannon's suggestion, I continued to watch Prophet Ugo Ezeji on Periscope. He talked about some of the things that were appearing in my dreams. For example, how people would be trying to force-feed me and touch me inappropriately. He explained that these types of dreams are bad because they mean that in the spirit realm the enemy was trying to get me to come to an agreement with it. After teaching on this subject, he then touched on the topic of witchcraft in dreams. I remembered some dreams where I was feverishly signing away at documents; Prophet Ugo Ezeji went on to explain that this was witchcraft.

Then he started praying deliverance prayers, at which point I began coughing up and feeling a little bit better. My dreams started getting better from this point on as well. I was gaining a lot of knowledge about deliverance, and I was excited to keep growing. I continued watching segments on Periscope and began following another deliverance ministry called Invicta Ministries. Like prophet Ugo, this minister would also pray deliverance prayers and I would throw up, or burp and pass gas a lot. These were some signs of deliverance.

Chapter 8

Heartsick

After a week of fasting and studying deliverance ministry, I had gained a lot of knowledge, but I still was not sensing God like I used to. That, paired with my husband talking to me almost daily and asking me to come home, made me wonder if all of this was just craziness. I was starting to doubt myself and what I had done. I knew I needed guidance and clarity – I knew I needed to call Peter and talk with him.

Around day eight of fasting I called Peter and explained to him all that was going on. We talked about why I left and how I believed I needed to leave my husband because of my promise with the angels. I didn't get into the dreams I'd been having, but I did tell him that I was not sensing God like I used to. I explained that I felt like I needed to get away and realign with God. Peter said he understood. He told me that he had the whole church praying and fasting for me to come back. I felt good about that. I told him I would think about it, but that I was still seeking God for clarity and understanding on what to do.

Even after I reconnected with Peter, I still felt unsure about everything. I tried to clear my mind by clearing the physical world in front of me. I worked on tidying my room – I even washed all my bedding and put nice, warm, clean sheets on my bed. I was excited to get some much needed rest, but when I fell asleep, I dreamt about Peter. He was coming close to me, and he was wearing farmer's clothing; he had on overalls with a basic T-shirt underneath. This dream took place on a farm inside a barn. I dreamt that he was coming close to me to have sex with me, but before it happened, my alarm went off.

I stayed in bed and got on the prayer line. I was praying, but it was very hard to stay awake – I was still so tired. The dream was so vivid, I felt myself going back to sleep and the dream trying to continue. To help me wake up, I decided to get on my knees and focus more on participating in the prayer line. Once I got on my knees with my face on the bed, I saw a big bug where I had been sleeping. I was startled, and I wondered how it was possible since I had just cleaned and changed all the bedding the night before. I tried to smash it, but it got away and I never saw it again. It disappeared into thin air. Somehow, I felt like it had something to do with my dream about Peter. As I continued to learn more I wondered if the bug was Peter. Could he have Shapeshifted into the bug to pursue me?

I continued on the prayer line, but I still was having a very difficult time staying awake. I ended up falling back asleep, and this time I dreamt I was in a room with Pastor Chris, my son Joseph, and my husband Bob. Then I saw Peter and he was much bigger than all of us. I dreamt he put his hand on Pastor Chris's head and started speaking to his head. Then he moved on to Joseph, and then to Bob. But I could not understand what he was saying to them. I woke back up at the very end of the prayer line meeting and tried to shift my focus on that. However, I still maintained some level of suspicion in my dreams and wanted to figure them out a little more.

Later that afternoon, I called Pastor Chris and I didn't know if he was okay – something seemed off. He said he had a headache, but we went ahead and talked a little about the dreams I had. However, the next day he was not on the prayer line like normal. I talked with him later that day and he said he still had a terrible headache, and he asked for prayers. I went on to speak with the Williams and my husband that day as well, and I started to think maybe I should go home. I hadn't begun looking for jobs yet, and I still did not sense God talking to me despite all this time spent fasting, worshipping, and praying. Bob informed me that he started meeting with Peter for some counseling at the church. He also informed me that Peter came over to the house and met with Joseph. It was good to hear, but in my heart I was still discontent. I told Bob, "Let me complete this ten-day fast and see if I hear anything from God."

The following day, I went to the store to get some necessities. I was weak because I had not had any food for nine days. As I was entering into a store, I saw an elderly woman walking as if she was in a lot of pain. I asked if I could pray for her and she said, "Oh yes, please!" So, I prayed for her back, her knee, and all her pain. She said that she had some anointing oil with her, and she put some on as I was praying. While I prayed, she started to speak in tongues. This was a sister in Christ. Once I finished praying, she said, "I am healed – I feel no pain." We exchanged numbers and after two weeks she gave me a phone call. She said she waited to call me to make sure the pain remained gone. She was so excited that she told her daughter and everyone in her prayer group about how the pain left her body and that she had been pain-free ever since. To God be the Glory!

Meanwhile, I was going through emotional turmoil. Upon completing the ten-day fast, Peter called me and told me, "Worship, then stop and listen to see what God is telling you." It turns out I actually had a vision, but I did not know it. I thought it was just my imagination, but I told Peter I had a thought where he and his wife were doing something strange. It was brief and vague, but I had seen it. He made no comment, but after a moment, asked me what I was going to do. I told him I still wasn't getting any specific words from God and that I would make my final decision tomorrow. That night, I had strange dreams as usual. I was frustrated, and I broke my fast. Why was I still having these dreams? Why could I not find the clarity I was so desperately seeking? Despite all my hard work, I did not get any revelation. My husband called me a little later and I told him I would come home.

The next day I went over to my sister's house and on the way there my car broke down. I thought maybe this was a sign that I was supposed to stay. My sister had been by my side through this entire journey – watching me go through the ups and downs, wondering if I was staying or going. We had many conversations over the past ten days, and I could tell that she was frustrated at this point. She said, "No, your car just broke down; this is not a sign. You need to go back home and be with your family." My husband was flying in the next day to drive me back home. He left first thing that morning, but the plane had multiple delays, so he didn't even get in until five or six that evening. So again, I started second-guessing everything.

Nevertheless, I felt committed to my decision to return home. I picked him up at the airport that evening and we drove from there to Pittsburgh. We spent the night in downtown Pittsburgh, and the next morning we set out on the second half of our trek back to Maryland. After two hours of driving, both of us felt so tired we were falling back asleep. He suggested I drive so he could rest and then we would switch turns. I told him I could barely keep my eyes open myself, so we pulled over at a rest area and took a nap. Even just napping, I was having very strange dreams. After we woke up from our nap we continued driving home.

Once we arrived home, my husband wanted me to call Peter to let him know I was home. I did, and Peter said he wanted to meet with us tomorrow for counseling. So, we met and I once again explained to them both that I still truly believed that Bob and I never should have been married. I reminded them of my very powerful dream where I promised I would get divorced by the time I turned thirty, and because I hadn't done this, I felt like I was missing my destiny. Peter went over scriptures about marriage and how God's word needs to take precedence over everything. He then advised that God is merciful and all is forgiven.

When I returned to church, people were welcoming, and told me they had been praying for me. They said that they were happy to see me back. I was glad to be back, truly. However, my dreams were getting worse again and very demonic. The following Sunday, Peter's wife, Lillian, was releasing her album of worship music. She told all the women to wear their blue African church dresses in celebration. When next Sunday came, I completely forgot to wear the dress that the Bishop's wife gave me, so I tried to stay out of sight and keep to myself.

Before Lillian went up before the church to sing, she and Peter were sitting with the other ministers and facing the congregation. There was a young Christian comedian there who was going to introduce her after his act. As he went on performing his comedy act, I noticed that Peter and his wife were sitting in their chairs strangely. They had their hands in a triangle. They had their hands between their legs with their thumbs touching each other and their index fingers touching each other, pointing downward in the shape of a triangle or pyramid.

https://www.google.com/amp/s/www.illuminatirex.com/ illuminati-signs/amp/

The pyramid is an important Illuminati symbol; it showcases their "few on the top ruling the many on the bottom" type power structure. The symbol becomes more powerful when the sign is done over an eye, representing the All-Seeing Eye in a capstone floating over an unfinished pyramid. The pyramid sign is seen by many researchers to be THE sign of the Illuminati.

https://www.google.com/amp/s/www.illuminatirex.com/ illuminati-signs/amp/

It was then that I recalled some of the YouTube videos on Satanic cults I had studied while I was in Ohio. I remembered that the triangle sign represented the Illuminati, which is a type of Satanic cult. After the young man was done performing his Christian comedian act, he introduced Lillian to perform songs from her new worship album. Something struck me – when she got up to sing, I noticed the way she was dressed was similar to what I saw in my vision. As she sang and moved around, I was reminded of the dream I had previously where a woman was performing, then she began to kiss a weak man but he sucked up her energy until she turned into a fish.

Lillian sang in French, and her album was in French too, so I couldn't understand any of it, but as she went around the church singing, she was making hand gestures. I noticed that the back-up singers were all making the hand signal that represents the devil's horn – where your pinky finger and your index finger are pointed up while your thumb and other fingers are pointed down. The back-up singers were making this symbol, and they were pointing their hands out to the audience while they sang.

https://www.google.com/amp/s/illuminatisymbols.info/spotting-illuminati-hand-signs-devils-horns-vs-ily-sign-vs-shaka-sign/amp/

The Devil's Horns hand symbol is known under many names including: Sign of the Horns, El Diablo, Sign of Satan the Horned God, the Goat, Goat Horns, Rock On, Rock Fist, The Horns, Mano Cornuto, Il Cornuto, Pommesgabel,

Evil Fingers, Metal Horns, Devil Sign, Diabolicus…

The Devil's Horns is one of the most widely recognized symbol of allegiance to Satan. The two raised fingers represent Satan's horns

https://www.google.com/amp/s/illuminatisymbols.info/spotting-illuminati-hand-signs-devils-horns-vs-ily-sign-vs-shaka-sign/amp/

The nice part about the videos that I watched back in Ohio about the Satanic signs and symbols. There was another hand gesture Lillian started to do which was called the cobwebs hand gesture. She was throwing her hand toward the audience and all her fingers were spread apart but slightly curled, like throwing a baseball with no baseball. I learned from the videos that this was casting a spell of cobwebs.

https://youtu.be/LqetEFdCqVE
https://youtu.be/AoR7rLr3rEw

I remembered watching a video on YouTube where this was used to curse the people with confusion. I thought to myself, maybe she just doesn't realize what she's doing. But then it dawned on me – Peter was raised in a satanic cult, so they would obviously know what they were doing. Once Lillian was done performing, she announced that she had copies of her album for sale. It was an open invitation to pay what you could. People were so excited to buy her

CD, and somebody even paid a thousand dollars for a copy. She said she wanted everybody to have a CD, and if they didn't bring money they could just pay her back later.

As I was getting ready to leave, I saw Esther's friend Tony across the room and went to talk to him. I let him know I was concerned about the hand signals I noticed during the performance, and that I was beginning to think this was not the church for me. Tony was skeptical, but I explained that she was making hand signals that represented the devil. She was also using a hand signal to put a spell on the audience. After some thought, he acknowledged what I said as valid. Tony and I had moved toward the door while we were talking, and one of Lillian's backup singers came up to us before we could leave and asked if we wanted to buy a CD.

Tony did take a copy of the album, but only gave a couple dollars for it. The backup singer then looked at me and asked me if I wanted to buy a CD. I declined. He asked me again and I firmly said, "I do not want one, thank you." He pushed back saying I could have it for free now and just pay later. I declined once more and turned to leave. As I was getting ready to exit the church, I could hear Peter at the front of the church, saying in a strong voice, "I want to introduce you all to Crystal – she's going to really help turn this church around." The exact same words he had said when he first brought me to his church. He asked her to come up to the front of the church, and she did. Then he had the church stretch out their hands toward her and pray for her. I then walked out of the church never to return again.

Chapter 9

New Beginnings

Unsure of what to do next, I reached out to the Williams and they set up a session with Pastor Chris for all of them to pray over me. We held the session at Pastor Chris's Church, and when they were praying over me, I began to vomit. It was a relief, but I knew I was not completely delivered. Pastor Chris was a busy man, so I didn't know how much more time we had, or how often he would be available to keep doing these sessions if needed. Honestly, I wasn't sure if he really understood all that I had gone through. Pastor Chris was more of a minister for faith rather than deliverance.

I took a chance and I got in touch with Invicta Ministries, www.invictaministries.org. Luckily, they were able to set up an appointment for me, and I was scheduled to have a deliverance session via Skype with their pastor – Pastor Mark. I explained to him what was going on. We talked in depth and I recounted as much detail as I could. When I got to the part about lending Peter's son a thousand dollars to fix his car, he interrupted me and said, "There you go – that was your initiation fee to join into witchcraft!"

Even to this day, I have never recovered any of that money. I told Mark all about the dreams of having sex with people. He asked me if I had received any jewelry in these dreams. I said yes! It was something I had never paid attention to before, but after putting some thought to it, I remembered that I was given rings and necklaces in these dreams. He told me to repeat after him: "I belong to Jesus Christ of Nazareth. I have nothing to do with spirit-husband. I reject the jewelry I have been given."

He told me to start ripping off the jewelry that I was given. This was a prophetic act; even though I could not physically see the jewelry on me, in the spirit realm I was giving the jewelry back to the evil spirits that gave them to me. He told me to start repeating after him again: "I reject you, I have nothing to do with witchcraft. I divorce you." He then instructed me to do another prophetic action and act like I was ripping up a piece of paper. I did, and I repeated after him, "I rip up this marriage certificate in the name of Jesus." Then Pastor Mark prayed over me. I truly felt like a weight was lifted off me.

This was the first time I finally understood that all I had dreamt was real in the spirit realm. I met with Pastor Mark a couple more times through Skype. In one of these sessions, I talked to him about the dream I had right before I got married, where angels came to me and told me that I wasn't supposed to marry Bob. I told him how I had come to an agreement with them that I would get divorced by the time I was thirty. Pastor Mark said he believed these were demons, not angels, and that they were trying to deceive me.

Later I learned through the church I am in now, New Beginning Ministries, when people in positions of authority state something negative to a person, this releases demons to try carry out what was spoken over them. When I was sixteen years old my parents and I visited my grandfather in a nursing home. He didn't really want to eat, and I was trying to feed him, but he got angry with me and said I would never get married because I was too aggressive. This statement could have been the open door which caused a curse to be placed on me.

Making this statement would give "legal rights" for demons to prevent me from getting married, and to cause that dream where the "angels" told me not to marry Bob. This can be confirmed by examining in the Bible where Noah and Abraham spoke blessings and curses over their children's lives that were played out through the rest of their lives and their descendants' lives. All this time I thought I made a vow to God, but it was only to demons. What a relief I felt upon learning this. After that deliverance session with Pastor Mark, his schedule was very busy, so it was hard to continue these sessions with him. Additionally, I was not working and it was encouraged to give a one-hundred dollar donation each time we met. So, I wasn't able to financially continue our sessions either. I had to look to God to help me on what to do next

Chapter 10

Finally Relief

I knew Jesus was Lord, and I prayed about where to go – asking God to lead me. Not long after, my friend Grace called me and said the church she recently started attending was having a prophetic conference that coming weekend. The church was called New Beginning Ministries. I laughed because if anybody needed a new beginning it was definitely me. The main minister there was a woman from Cameroon named Paulette and the associate minister was a woman from Nigeria named Eniolade. Then there was a male minister from Nigeria, who lived in Wisconsin. He was called Reverend Baba-Lola. That night, the first time I attended, he prophesied over everyone.

Overall, it was a positive experience. There was a lot of praise and worship happening, and many people were being prophesied over. I spoke to the ministers there and I scheduled a deliverance session for myself. I was to meet in a week and half on a Thursday. I was told to fast three days prior to coming, but I fasted for seven days because I wanted to make sure everything that I'd been exposed to would be gone. That next Wednesday, the day before my deliverance, I dreamt I was going to the bathroom all over the place and all of this waste was just flowing out of me. I knew this was a dream of deliverance. Thank God!

I felt like God was showing me that I didn't need to always seek help by going to people for deliverance – I only needed to go to Him. He alone is able to deliver me. The next day I went to New Beginning Ministries and I told the ministers Paulette and Eniolade about the dream I had. They both said that I had been delivered but they would pray over me anyway. I felt so much relief, and I noticed I had started to sense Jesus next to me again. In fact, I later had a vision of Him giving me daisies. I chalked this up to my imagination, but when I went to church the following Thursday evening, Paulette came to pray over me and said, "I see you're receiving flowers." I was amazed; I hadn't told her about my vision. Then I knew it was not my imagination – I truly was seeing Jesus giving me daisies. God was back in my life again, and I continued to attend New Beginning Ministries.

About a year and half later, I sensed God telling me to write this book. However, I thought nobody's going to believe me about all this crazy stuff. I knew I needed confirmation rather than just a sense that this was meant to be. God gave me two confirmations. The first one was with Reverend Baba-Lola. I started having some of my nightmares again after a while, seemingly out of the blue. I didn't know what was going on, but as soon as this started happening, Reverend Baba-Lola was in town again prophesying over people. I knew I needed to see him as soon as possible.

When I did, he started praying over me with Reverend Eniolade. He said something had flown into my life from a man that he saw. He said it was an African man, and then he described Peter. Reverend Baba-Lola had no knowledge of my past, but he saw into my life. He said, "This man is where your dreams are coming from." I was instructed to go through my house and get rid of absolutely anything associated with Peter and his church. I had already thrown out the dress and CD I had, and I couldn't think of anything else they had given me. But at the request of the reverend, I went through my house again. I found a song book from Peter's church. It was tucked in with some other books and on the shelf behind my bed. I threw it away and the dreams subsided.

A few months later, Reverend Paulette had a dream about what was happening in Peter's church. She let me know that what I was going through was true. She said she dreamt of a demonic well in the church, and the Holy Spirit showed her that souls were trapped in it. She said the dream was very scary and she told the Holy Spirit she did not want to see any more of it. I believe she was only shown a glimpse of what was going on, but it was enough to make her believe. She had known Peter and his wife for years, and I think she really didn't know what to believe about my story at first, until she had this dream. God confirmed it and showed her the truth.

The other confirmation I received was through a question I had for God; I asked him about the homeless friends I had made – I wanted to know if they were really sent from Him or not. I asked God, "If they are truly from you, Lord, I ask that I will see them again soon." They had stopped living at the bus stop they resided at for years, and I hadn't seen them in a while. On multiple occasions, I tried calling them at the phone numbers they had given me previously, but these numbers were no longer in service. Two days later, Bob and I took the metro to downtown D.C. to visit his mom. As soon as we got on, we saw Esther, Moses and

Debra. I was elated! I told them I had just prayed to God about them, and that it was no coincidence we ran into each other. I started to pray over them. I asked for God to restore and heal them.

You may be reading this book and thinking this is far-fetched. If so, I ask you these questions: Are you going through something? Is your family going through some-thing that you know is not where God wants your lives to be? Do you know in your heart that you are not living out your destiny? Are you having dreams where you seem to be wandering around, lost? Are you having sexual dreams, dreams where you're being attacked, or dreams where you're eating non-stop? Are there open doors in your life that need closed? If so, I would encourage you to examine the details of your own life to see if you may have fallen victim to witchcraft, general curses, or other sins. I my-self would have thought these events were far-fetched if I hadn't gone through them first-hand. These instances creep upon us, and we may not know until it's too late. Take stock of what's going on in your life and decide if you too may need to go through deliverance.

Prayer Section

Before coming to God in prayer, one needs to recognize that Jesus died on the cross for our sins and the only way we can approach God is through Jesus Christ. According to Romans 10:9 (KJV), that if you confess with your mouth the Lord Jesus and believe in your heart that God has raised him from the dead, you will be saved.

The first step before praying is really to confess that Jesus is lord, and truly believe it in your heart. Personally, I like to sing to God and worship him before I start praying to him. This helps me feel more connected to him. I also start to sense his presence and manifestation. The second step is to repent of your sins and search in your heart the things you know you've done wrong.

"If we confess our sins, he is faithful and just to forgive us our sins, and to cleanse us from all unrighteousness." 1 John 1:9 KJV

With that being said, according to the word of God it is important to be baptized if you have not been. However, this should not prevent you from praying for redemption.

"Then Peter said unto them, repent, and be baptized every one of you in the name of Jesus Christ for the remission of sins, and ye shall receive the gift of the Holy Ghost. 39For the promise is unto you, and to your children, and to all that are afar off, even as many as the Lord our God shall call." Acts 2:38-39 KJV

After repenting you should start praying to break soul ties with unhealthy people in your life. In the book, Breaking the Power of Familiar Spirits: How to Deal with Demonic Conspiracies, by Kimberly Daniels. She explains that souls can be tied to one another - using 1 Samuel 18:1 as an example. That verse states that Jonathan loved David as himself, that Jonathan was bonded to the soul of David. "Soul" comes from the Hebrew "nephesh," meaning sentience, as it relates to passions and man's emotion (4).

Should you be affected by someone that is working with the kingdom of darkness, then you must pray to break the soul tie. First, physically separate from them, then pray this simple prayer: "I cut the soul tie with (say the person's name). In Jesus' name, Amen."

Say it a few times. You can also break a soul tie with a group of people or even a physical object. It could be a specific church, or the members of that church. It could be a gift that was given to you by the person that you're trying to break the soul tie. This is particularly important if you know they were practicing witchcraft or anything occult.

One of my favorite prayers that help me break off any evil effects of the kingdom of darkness is from a YouTube video by prophet Ugo Ezeji. With this prayer you will need anointing oil. If you do not have anointing oil, Ugo will guide you through a prayer asking God to bless oil that you do have on hand (starting at 18:30). That prayer will ask God and the Holy Spirit to touch the oil so that it may bring forth deliverance and healing. I place oil on two paper plates and stand on them to avoid a big mess. Be careful while doing so.

To pray along with Ugo Ezeji, start the video at twenty-two minutes.

"In the name of Jesus. Today is the day of freedom. As we take part of this prophetic action, let your people be set free. In the name of Jesus as I stand on this oil, I disconnect myself from the demonic realm. As I stand on this oil, I disconnect myself from every power of darkness that is following me. In the name of Jesus as I stand on the oil, I make myself untraceable to every spiritual wickedness that has been calling out my name. As I stand upon this oil, every alter that has been speaking against me, be completely dismantled. As I stand on this oil, I declare in the name of Jesus I am surrounded by the fire of the Holy Spirit. That familiar spirit will not be able to find me. And the spirit of death shall pass over me. I stand upon this oil, I surround myself with the fire of the Holy Ghost. That where so ever I walk I will not walk alone but I walk with the angels of God. As I stand upon this oil, I walk away from my past. I step out of my past, My past afflictions, my past weaknesses, my past shortcomings, my past sicknesses and diseases, my past doubt, and my past unbelief, as I stand on this oil I stand on the word of God. I stand in faith and a new level of strength I declare strength to be released to my legs and my knees that, I will walk this walk and run this race. As I stand up on the oil I declare newness of life I

will leap over walls and run through the troops in
Jesus is mighty name amen. Today is the day of
freedom, today is the day of deliverance in the name
of Jesus, Amen."

Here is another helpful prayer point that helps break generational curses. These are caused by our ancestors' sins and transgressions. For example, when they sinned, transgressed, or came into a covenant with the kingdom of darkness. Because our ancestors are no longer living, these demons, devils can be passed down to us. Their job is to influence us to participate in the kingdom of darkness.

To do this I refer to *Prayers that Rout Demons*
by John Eckhardt.

"I am redeemed from the curse of the law.
I break all generational curses of pride, lust,
perversion, rebellion, witchcraft, idolatry, poverty,
rejection, fear, confusion, addiction, death, and
distraction in the name of Jesus.
I command all generational spirits that came into
my life during conception, in the womb, in the birth
canal, and through umbilical cord to come out in
the name of Jesus.
I break all spoken curses and negative words that I
have spoken over myself in the name of Jesus.
I break all spoken curses and negative words
spoken over my life by others, including those in
authority in the name of Jesus.
I command all hereditary spirits of lust, Projection,

fear, sickness, infirmity, common disease, anger, hatred, confusion, failure in poverty to come out of my life in the name of Jesus.

I break the legal rights of all generational spirits operating behind a curse in the name of Jesus. You have

no legal right to operate in my life.

I bind and rebuke all familiar spirit and spirit guides that would try to operate in my life from my ancestors in the name of Jesus.

I renounce all false beliefs and philosophies inherited by my ancestors in the name of Jesus.

I break all curses of sickness and disease and command all inherited sicknesses to leave my body in the name of Jesus. Through Jesus, my family is blessed.

I renounce all pride inherited from my ancestors in the name of Jesus.

I break all oaths, vows, and packs made with the Devil by my ancestors in the name of Jesus.

I break all curses by agents of Satan spoken against my life in secret in the name of Jesus.

I break all written curses that would affect my life in the name of Jesus.

I break every time released curse that would activate in my life as I grow older in the name of Jesus.

I break every curse Balaam against my life in the name of Jesus. Lord, turn every curse spoken against my life into a blessing.

I break all generational rebellion that would cause me to resist the Holy Spirit.

I break all curses of death spoken by people in

authority in my Nation over my nation in the name of Jesus.
I break curses of death spoken against America by people from other nations in the name of Jesus" (22).

After that I ended the prayer from the Eckhardt book. I will then command in the name of Jesus anything and everything that is not of God you need to go to the dry place

and be bound and banished there in the name of Jesus and ask the Holy Spirit to fill me up. I start thanking and praising Jesus for the deliverance.

To round out this prayer session I look to Confessions Against Spirit-Husband by Rev. Emmanuel Baba-Lola. This is a passage where you will give all that you are over to God and use his glory to denounce and distance yourself from Satan. In this prayer you also ask God to protect you from ancestral curses by rooting you in his righteousness

.

"I (put your name) am a property of Jesus Christ; I am bought at the price of His precious shed-blood. He is my Savior, my only Savior; my one and only Lord, Master, and all in all. I am crucified with Christ and I no longer live. The life I now live in the body, I live by the faith of the Son of God who loved me and gave Himself for me. I stand on the Word of God; I stand in the grace of my Lord

Jesus Christ and thrive on it. The tender mercies of God is the crown that adorns my head. I stand in my inheritance in Christ. My life is preserved, protected, and hidden in Christ. I am seated in Christ at the right hand of the Lord, Most High; far above all principalities and powers, and every name that is named. From this vantage position as an heir of God and joint heir with Christ, I am now speaking.

I speak as one that is one spirit with the Lord and as a partaker of His divine nature. I stand in my authority in Christ as the one holding forth for Christ on earth until He returns. I decree and I declare that there is absolutely no power of Satan over me. Therefore, I speak in His name, the almighty name of Jesus Christ that is all powerful in heaven, on Earth, and in Hell.

The Devil is my footstool and I hereby spit on his face. I refute the Devil, I denounce him, renounce him, and reject him absolutely and will never recognize him. He is filthy and stinking; I have nothing to do with him as light has nothing to do with darkness. I break the power of Satan over my mind; I do not permit him to speak to me, touch me in anyway or come near me. I destroy the power of Satan over my spirit and body; I am the Temple of the Holy Spirit. I am a Prince/Princess of the Kingdom of God ably defined as 'Righteousness, peace, and joy in the Holy Spirit.' Therefore, the righteousness of Christ is mine, the inexhaustible peace of God is

*my right, and the amazing joy of the Holy Spirit is
my benefit. I do not stand in my own righteousness;
I have none. I do not earn my peace; Jesus Christ
my Savior paid for it. The joy of the Holy Spirit flows
in me by grace; it is independent from my
circumstances. Therefore, I rebuke you Satan;
depart from me! You cannot and will not disinherit
me from my rights in the Kingdom of God, my Father.
I am standing in the righteousness of Christ; you have
no basis to accuse me. The peace of God in my life
is Christ's promise faithfully kept; you will not rob
me of it as my Savior does not eat his words. The joy
of the Holy Spirit is a river that flows from my
belly; you are incompetent to stop it. I confess,
affirm, and declare: my rights as a beloved
Son/daughter of God cannot be threatened. I know
you are a thief, a murderer, and a destroyer but I am
not your prey. I am a victor and more than a
conqueror; I am light and you are darkness. My
ungodly past and ancestry are the reasons I need a
savior and I have the Savior—the Lord Jesus Christ.
I am a wild olive branch cut-off and grafted into
God's olive tree; I share in the nourishing sap from
the olive root of Abraham. Therefore, I am cut-off
and protected from ancestral curses and inherited
liabilities.*

*The devil is my footstool; I tread on the lion and the
cobra; I trample the great lion and the serpent. It
is fruitless to attack me; no weapon forged against
me prosper and I am a judge over every tongue that*

accuses me. This is my heritage and vindication as a servant of the Lord from whom my righteousness flows.

I am not ignorant of the devices of Satan; therefore, you, Satan cannot take any advantage of me. I am not ignorant that I, a daughter of Zion, has nothing to do with spirit-husband; according to the word of God. I am a child of God; I don't accept ancestral covenants or burdens of errors already paid for in full by the finished work of Christ, my beloved Lord and Savior. Therefore, I renounce you, you foul spirit parading yourself as my spirit-husband. I command you to depart from me because you are under my feet and eternally beneath me as a child of God. My life is hidden with Christ; you cannot mess with it. You do not have my permission to touch me in anyway or do anything about me. I decree and I declare that you get away from me permanently forever; in Jesus' almighty name."

Reference Page

Baba-Lola, Emmanuel. "Confession Against the 'Spirit-Husband.'" Emmanuel Baba-Lola's Blog, 2019, acts1038.com/confession-against-the-spirit-husband/.

"Cobweb Attack Prayer." YouTube, Star International Ministry, 13 July 2018, youtu.be/LqetEFdCqVE.

Daniels, Kimberly. Breaking the Power of Familiar Spirits: How to Deal with Demonic Conspiracies. Charisma House, 2018.

Eckhardt, John. Prayers That Rout Demons. Charisma House, 2008.

Ezeji, Ugo. "Deliverance Unveiled The Weapon of Oil." YouTube, 8 Nov. 2016, youtu.be/pkMqzfI1h00.

Franklin, Jentezen. Fasting: Opening the Door to a Deeper, More Intimate, More Powerful Relationship with God. Charisma House, 2014.

Goodman, Elisha. Prayer Cookbook for Busy People (Book 4): Cracking Your Dream Code. Elisha Goodman, 2009.

Isigi, Christine. "Powerful Prayer to Crush Demonic Cobwebs Spider Attacks. Prophetess Christine Isigi." YouTube, Overcomers DHMinistries TV, 27 Oct. 2016, youtu.be/AoR7rLr3rEw.

LeClaire, Jennifer. The Spiritual Warrior's Guide to Defeating Water Spirits: Overcoming Demons That Twist, Suffocate, and Attack God's Purposes for Your Life. Destiny Image Publishers, Inc., 2018.

Olukoya, D. K. Disgracing Water Spirits: Deliverance Manual for Indigenes of Riverine Areas. Mountain of Fire and Miracles Ministries, 2012.

Simpson, Tialie. Urban Disciples: A Guidebook. Blurb, 2020.

Thompson, Adam F., and Adrian Beale. The Divinity Code to Understanding Your Dreams and Visions. Destiny Image, 2011.

www.ingramcontent.com/pod-product-compliance
Lightning Source LLC
La Vergne TN
LVHW021349080426
835508LV00020B/2190